HOW TO MASTER
THE ART OF
WRITING
CHILDREN'S
BOOKS

Bobbie Hinman

How to Master the Art of Writing Children's Books

ISBN: 978-1-7365459-3-5 (sc) | 978-1-7365459-6-6 (hc)
        978-1-7365459-5-9 (e)

Library of Congress Control Number: 2021916399

Publisher's Cataloging-in-Publication data

Names: Hinman, Bobbie, author.
Title: How to master the art of writing children's books / Bobbie Hinman.
Description: Includes index. | Kissimmee, FL: Best Fairy Books, 2021.
Identifiers: LCCN: 2021916399 | ISBN: 978-1-7365459-3-5 (sc) | 978-1-7365459-6-6 (hc) | 978-1-7365459-5-9 (e)
Subjects: LCSH Children's literature--Authorship. | Children--Books and reading. | Creative writing. | BISAC LANGUAGE ARTS & DISCIPLINES / Writing / Children's & Young Adult | LANGUAGE ARTS & DISCIPLINES / Writing / Authorship
Classification: LCC PN147.5 .H56 2021 | DDC 808/.068--dc23

Best Fairy Books
www.bestfairybooks.com

*I dedicate this book to you,
my zealous writers.*

*The harder you work, I promise,
the luckier you will become.*

Enjoy your journey.

Table of Contents

Part 5. How to Write a Rhyming Story

Part 6. Tend to More Details

Part 7. Revise and Perfect Your Manuscript

Part 8. A Few Last Words

Introduction

Writing is an Art

When we think of *the arts,* we often think of painting, sculpting, and even dancing. Writing isn't something that always comes to mind. According to the Merriam-Webster dictionary, art is *the use of creativity, skill, and imagination to create something that's beautiful or emotionally expressive.* Yes, writing is an art, and as with any other art, hard work and determination are required if you wish to achieve success.

Each of us is on this journey for a different reason:

- Perhaps you are interested in writing a children's book, but don't know where to begin.

- You may be a seasoned writer looking to refresh your writing skills.

- Maybe you are yearning to write a book, but a lack of confidence is holding you back.

- Perhaps you have been told that there are simply a few numbered steps to take to create the perfect book, but that hasn't worked out.

- Maybe you simply have a story or memory that you have dreamed of sharing with the world.

Whatever the reason, you have come to the right place.

I wish I could tell you that writing a book is easy. I wish I could offer you 7, or 10, or even 20 magic steps to follow to miraculously produce a bestseller. But the truth is, it takes an enormous amount of work and a real dedication. And even then, your success is not guaranteed. But what will help, and is perhaps the hardest part, is making the decision to master the art of writing.

My writing career began over 40 years ago. A lot has changed since I wrote my first book with pen and paper, then typed it on a…typewriter! But this doesn't mean that having the internet at your fingertips is going to make the process a breeze. When choosing any path in life, the best way to start is to research your chosen field, take at least a few courses—and study a lot. Then comes practice, practice, practice. The art of writing is no different.

Learning builds self-confidence. For you, my fellow writers, whether you are seasoned authors or novices, I have compiled this reference book to offer a roadmap that will give you the basic writing skills, build your confidence, activate your imagination, and guide you along your journey. If your journey has already begun, this book will fill in the gaps as you hone your writing skills.

Whether you are self-publishing your book, or plan to submit your manuscript to a traditional publisher or literary agent, you will need to present the best story possible. The information I am offering you will help you make that great first impression.

There is a lot to learn if this is the path you choose to follow. I know how hard it is because I have been traveling this journey for many years. My goal now is to help *you* get there. If you wish to write a successful children's book, this may be the most important book you will ever read.

Can you do it? Of course you can. *Will* you do it? It's up to you.

"You can do anything in life you want; you just have to want to do it."

—My mom

PART 1

Ready...Set...
Begin

1

So You Want to Write a Children's Book?

Do you want to write a book? Let me tell you a secret: Anyone can write a book. And here's another secret: Only a skillful writer can write a *good* book—one that is well-written, memorable and entertaining. But before you pick up your pencil or open your laptop, you might want to ask yourself the following question:

"Why do I want to write a book?"

People write books for a number of reasons:

Do you have a unique story to tell? Each of us has adventures, either small or large, every day. Some of us recognize the adventures; others do not. It's similar to carrying a camera wherever you go. Some people will take amazing photos of children playing, people smiling, butterflies flitting, planes flying by—each simple photo expressing its own message. Others will notice none of life's actions, failing to recognize that they are even experiencing an adventure. Those of us with imagination will make our memories indelible by becoming writers.

Do you have an educational or moral lesson to share? As we grow, we learn. How wonderful it is to have accumulated knowledge about a subject. Perhaps your background in finance will enable you to teach children to manage their money. Perhaps your career as a therapist will help you guide children along the path to believing in themselves. For many teachers, the lessons they have learned could fill volumes. Many of us have gained wisdom from life itself. This may now be your time to impart your knowledge to others.

Do you know a child, or an animal—or even an object (like a very generous Giving Tree) that would make a perfect main character? Most of us know a child with a knack for doing outlandish things, or perhaps we have a pet who is an escape artist. Almost any silly or humorous incident can be developed into a story that children will enjoy. For example, I may someday tell the story of my son's nighttime adventures with "the man wearing bandaids all over his body." It took us quite a while to figure out that our son was watching late-night horror movies while everyone else was asleep.

Are you one of the lucky adults who still believes in magic and fantasy? If so, you may want to be a part of the magical world where animals wear clothes and zombies live in the classroom at night, or where kittens ride in spaceships and fairies visit children while they sleep. Children still believe, so go for it!

Do you want to put something in writing for your family? Many of us have stories or histories that we wish to pass on to future generations—perhaps a memoir to be cherished or a poem to be written. This can be a beautiful gift to your friends, family—and yourself.

Do you think writing a children's book will be a simple task?
Many people think that writing for children is easy. Children's books are short and simple—and they're for children. Right? So how hard can that be? Please remember this: You will have to appeal to the reader (the child) and also the person with the purse strings! Writing for two audiences often makes children's books more difficult to write than other genres. Besides, you will have to know how children think and how they process information.

Is this where you will make your fortune? If your reason for writing is to amass a fortune, I'm sorry to burst your bubble. If making money is your only goal, you might want to find a new route to wealth. In some cases, writing *can* become a lucrative additional income, but it's rarely an easy path.

Understanding your motivation to write will help you choose your target audience and focus your energies. A clear vision and goal will afford you the drive and endurance to succeed.

"If there's a book that you want to read, but it hasn't been written yet, then you must write it."
                                        —Toni Morrison

2

Understand What Children Like to Read

The famous children's author, C.S. Lewis, when asked how to write for children, answered:

> *"Children are, of course, a special public and you must find out what they want and give them that, however little you like it yourself."*

The most important part of this statement is, *find out what they want.* This is why I always advise authors to *read, read, read!* If you want to please your audience, you must find out what children like—and just as importantly—what they *don't* like.

What Children Like

Children like to believe in make-believe.
Children have great imaginations. They believe in fairies and aliens, and they love things that are silly and quirky, such as cars that talk and chickens that fly to the moon. Children still believe that these things can happen. Fairy tales will never go out of style if we let children *believe* as long as possible.

Even Albert Einstein understood the need for make-believe when he said, "If you want your children to be intelligent, read them fairy tales. If you want them to be more intelligent, read them more fairy tales." One of your goals as a children's book author should be to write a book that children will want to read over and over.

Children like identifiable characters & situations.
Children like to read about the things that interest them, often picturing themselves as characters from a story. After reading a book, if a youngster pretends to be one of the characters—perhaps trying to fly around the room, or talking to the fairy that they insist lives under their bed—there's a good chance they are successfully identifying with a character from the story.

Children like illustrations.
This is important to keep in mind when writing for children. Choose the type of illustrations that are suitable for your target age group—large spot illustrations for *board books* (books for toddlers), full page illustrations for *picture books*, and fewer illustrations (or even none at all) as you target older children in middle-grade novels. Whatever type of book you write, keep in mind that children are attracted to bright colors and action-filled illustrations. Aside from being nice to look at, illustrations should *add* to the story, perhaps giving details that aren't explicitly stated in the text.

Children like happy endings.
Children feel good when a situation is resolved and the characters *live happily ever after*. This is one reason why bedtime stories are always popular. Happy thoughts before going to sleep are a luxury to be cherished. Young children are emotionally

vulnerable and need a satisfying conclusion. This does not mean that they should avoid reading stories about unpleasant issues, such as divorce or losing a loved one; but these topics need to be handled skillfully, leaving young readers with a feeling of hope.

Children like having something to look forward to.
They like the anticipation that comes from reading a book and knowing that the characters they are identifying with will reappear on the next page, or even in another book. This is why book series are often so successful. It is also the reason why well-written chapter books hold the interest of young readers, who love the suspense of not knowing what predicament the character will get into next.

Children like cliffhangers.
It's important to have the words and illustrations on each page of a picture book create curiosity in young readers and pique their interest in learning what will happen on the next page. If the book is part of a series, children will be more likely to *stay tuned* if the story ends with a bit of a hook, or hint, about what is coming in the next book.

Chapter books offer even more opportunities for cliffhangers. Each chapter needs to end in a way that makes the reader curious about what will happen next and anxious to turn the page to the next chapter. Young readers need something to look forward to.

Often a simple statement or question will work at the end of a page or chapter. You can also use punctuation to add to the drama. Often an exclamation mark or ellipsis will do the trick, though be careful not to overuse either one.

Examples of anticipatory endings:
- My hunt is about to lead me to a real dinosaur egg!
- Suddenly the door opened...
- He couldn't believe what he saw.
- She walked up the crooked lane to the spooky house, then...
- I think I have it—the last clue!
- What is Grandpa hiding in this treasure box?

What Children DON'T Like

Children don't like being preached to or scolded.
One way to be sure you are not coming across as *preachy* is to express your message through your character's dialogue and actions rather than your own narrative. Children learn by watching the mistakes of other children and the way these mistakes are dealt with. They shy away from lessons that are dictated to them by grownups—or unseen narrators.

Children understand simple concepts.
It's imperative to be familiar with the comprehension level of your readers. Stating broad concepts is often useless when writing for children.

Example of a broad concept:
When Jamie gave his toys away, he felt happiness spread across the world.

This may be a beautiful thought; but for a young child, more understanding will likely be gained by using the words: *Jamie gave his toys away and was happy knowing that he was making other children happy too.*

Other examples of broad concepts that are vague and are better understood if explained more simply:

- *The answer to who we are lies within each of us.*
- *If you are courageous, you will find your true self.*
- *Don't blame the judgement of others.*
- *Giving and sharing will make love radiate from your heart.*

Children don't always want to learn a lesson.
Not every book has to teach a moral lesson. Young children read for enjoyment, so if we want them to read more, let's allow them the joy of disappearing into the world of fantasy and fun. The more they enjoy reading, the more they will want to read.

Many of us have heard stories of *reluctant reader*s who became obsessed with the *Harry Potter* series and were totally captivated by its magical themes. Joyfully, millions of children (and grownups) read all seven books, not intimidated at all by the number of pages in each volume.

Keep in mind that it's imperative to write a well-structured story with a beginning, middle and end, as well as interesting characters and meaningful dialogue. More on all of these topics later!

"Words are our most inexhaustible source of magic."

— J.K. Rowling

3

Types of Children's Books

The type of book you choose to write will depend on the age group you are targeting, or conversely, the age group you choose may help you determine what type of book to write. Either way, it's a good idea to visit your local library and take a look at the different types of books. Then choose the type that appeals to you.

It's important to note that there is slight disagreement in the literary community when it comes to the specific age breakdown for each type of book. For example, some sources list ages 3 to 8 for picture books; others list ages 3 to 7, 4 to 7, or 4 to 8. There are also varying opinions when it comes to word count. One reason for the disparity in numbers is that the gaining popularity of self-published books has given writers the flexibility to create their own rules. Traditionally-published books (sometimes via an agent who helps sell it to a publisher) generally follow traditionally-established rules that are not mandatory for self-published authors. As a result, self-publishing offers the author more creative control over the book's content, length and appearance.

Knowing that opinions vary, keep in mind that reading ability also varies within each category. Parents and teachers will ultimately choose the books that are suitable for their children.

The general categories of children's books are:

Board books
For children ages 18 months to 3 years, *board books* are printed on very heavy stock to meet the demands of active little ones who like to tear pages and chew on corners. The illustrations, brightly colored and simple, are the most important element in these books. There is no real story or plot. Board books can have either no words, a few words, or simple sentences. Popular topics may include shapes, colors, animals (usually more common types, such as puppies, kittens or bunnies), or children doing simple tasks, like brushing their teeth or putting on a hat and mittens.

Board books typically contain 12 to 18 pages (6 to 9 two-sided boards). The dimensions of a board book are typically 6 inches x 6 inches.

An example of an all-time favorite board book is *Brown Bear, Brown Bear, What Do You See?* by Bill Martin, Jr.

Wordless books
A relatively little-known subcategory of children's books, *wordless books* tell a story without words, using only illustrations as guidance. This allows the readers to create the stories that they are imagining as they follow the illustrations. These books offer an excellent pre-literacy activity that encourages the use of imagination. Creating a book without words is much harder than it sounds. The author and the illustrator need to create meaningful action on each page and be able to show the characters' mindset through the use of facial expressions.

Wordless books can be in the form of board books or picture books; the format you choose will be your guideline for deciding on the dimensions and page count.

One excellent example of a successful wordless book is *Good Dog, Carl* by Alexandra Day.

Picture books

For children ages 4 to 8, *picture books* are books in which the pictures are as important as the words. The illustrations have the important job of helping to tell the story. The illustrations offer details that the text may not cover, thus adding to the richness of the characters and plot. Picture books that rhyme are among the favorites of children in this age group.

There is one main plot in a picture book, and there are no subplots; however, the information offered by the illustrations can sometimes be considered a subplot of its own. For example, you don't have to use words to say that Billy's little brother does everything that Billy does; you can show Billy's brother imitating him in every illustration. In this way, the pictures become vital to the storyline.

Picture book stories can be either fiction or non-fiction. Traditionally, these books contain 32 pages and between 200 and 800 words. They can be printed in a variety of sizes, some of the most popular being 8.5 inches x 8.5 inches, 10 inches x10 inches, and 8.5 inches x 11 inches (landscape orientation).

An example of a popular children's picture book written in prose is *If You Give a Mouse a Cookie* by Laura Numeroff. A popular picture book written in rhyme is *Sheep in a Jeep* by Nancy Shaw.

Coloring and activity books

These books are creating excitement and becoming quite popular, adding an entirely new dimension to the reading experience. They are extremely popular among the 4 to 8 age group; however, they can be written for *any* age range. Activity books are relatively inexpensive to produce and, as a companion to an existing book, can be a great marketing tool. Aside from offering pages to color, these books often contain activities involving reading and math that enable children to expand their academic skills.

The page count for activity books can be determined by the writer and based on the target age group. The average dimensions of an activity book varies from 6 inches x 9 inches for puzzle books geared toward older children, to 8.5 inches x 11 inches (portrait orientation) in coloring books for the younger ages.

Picture storybooks

For children ages 7 to 9, *picture storybooks* are similar in style to picture books, but have more words and sometimes fewer illustrations; nevertheless, the text and pictures still work together to tell the story. The plots and characters can be slightly more complex than those in picture books, and simple subplots may be used. At this age, children are interested in both fiction and non-fiction books, yet still love fantasy and humor, with *bathroom humor* being among their favorites. Picture storybooks contain from 32 pages to 64 pages, and up to 2000 words.

A popular picture storybook is *The Day I Swapped My Dad for Two Goldfish* by Neil Gaiman.

Early readers

For children ages 6 to 8 who are almost ready to transition from picture books to chapter books, *early readers* offer stories in a format geared to children who are able to read by themselves. Early readers are usually divided into small chapters. If you are writing an early reader, the key is to use age-appropriate vocabulary, along with smaller illustrations than those found in picture books. It's also important to understand that, although early readers contain illustrations, they are not simply longer picture books. They are designed to target individual reading levels and, because of this, are often more difficult to write. If you choose this path, you will need to research Lexile and vocabulary levels so you can tag your book with an accurate reading level.

Early readers are almost always in paperback format, typically 5.5 inches x 8 inches. They contain from 35 to 50 pages, and up to 1700 words.

Note: Lexile scores are available for every type of book. The Lexile score measures the difficulty of a book and is based on a combination of age and grade level. Educators rely on these levels when choosing appropriate books for their students; a book with a high score will be more difficult to understand than a book with a low score. (If you would like more information about Lexile scores, or would like to obtain a score for your book, visit Lexile.com.)

Chapter books

For children ages 8 to 10 who are able to read independently, *chapter books* fall between early readers and middle grade books. Chapter books have longer, more involved stories to tell.

Unlike picture books that have one plot, chapter books contain several subplots.

Action is important in chapter books. The plots and characters will need to create enough excitement and action to carry the reader from chapter to chapter. There is no hard and fast age rule, and there are no cut-off dates for children to make the transition to chapter books. Many children are ready for chapter books at age 8, but this transition depends largely on each child's reading ability.

Early chapter books usually have from 5,000 to 15,000 words and fewer illustrations than books geared to younger readers.

An example of a popular chapter book is the *Captain Underpants* series by Dav Pilkey.

Middle grade books

For children ages 8 to 12, middle grade books are the next step after chapter books. This may sound confusing because middle grade books are also divided into chapters. The difference is that chapter books are more simplistic; middle grade books deal with more complicated subjects and more intricate plots and subplots. Action is still important, however these books go a step further, adding a lot more description. Middle grade books are generally geared to strong readers.

These books can have from 20,000 to 60,000 words. They contain few, if any, illustrations.

The best example of a middle grade book is the *Harry Potter* series by J.K. Rowling.

Graphic novels

For children ages 12 and up (with some written for ages 16 to 18, and even adults), graphic novels are a growing category of books. These books are similar to comic books, but are longer and more complex and are often offered as part of a series. They follow the general story guidelines of having a well-developed character and a beginning, middle and end, but the storytelling relies more on the illustrations than the words. The text is shown primarily in word bubbles, rather than the typical sentence and paragraph format used in other types of children's books. We often think of *graphic novels* as fantasy or horror books, but they include many genres, encompassing both fiction and non-fiction categories.

Graphic novels can have from 48 pages to several hundred pages, and therefore take much longer to illustrate than most other books.

One example of a bestselling graphic novel is *Minecraft* by R. Sfé Monster.

Note: It's important to understand that you cannot simply change the type of book you are writing based on its page count. For example, if a picture book ends up with 2500 words, you cannot automatically turn it into a chapter book. Follow the guidelines above—and be sure to do your research.

"It is the writer who might catch the imagination of young people, and plant a seed that will flower and come to fruition."
—Isaac Asimov

4

Know Your Target Audience

Before you can write a story that will appeal to your target audience, you need to decide *who* comprises that audience. If you are writing for toddlers and preschoolers, the vocabulary and level of detail will not be the same as if you are writing for first and second graders.

New authors often see their books as *all inclusive*, thinking the books will please every child between the ages of 3 and 10. Connecting with such a broad audience takes very skillful writing, and there are very few authors who can accomplish this feat. There is a vast difference in comprehension, interest and attention span between toddlers and fourth graders. The youngest readers in a wide target audience would understandably feel frustrated by books that are too difficult, while older readers would likely be bored by books that are too simplistic.

The way you develop your story will depend on the specific age group you decide to target. For example, a story about dinosaurs written for toddlers would contain bright, simple drawings of comical dinosaurs, vastly different from a story about dinosaurs written for second or third graders, which would contain more realistic illustrations and details about the way dinosaurs lived.

Read. Read. Read.
Once you have decided on your target audience, I
can't stress enough the importance of reading as
many books as possible that are written for that age
group. As you read, take special note of the theme,
length of sentences, vocabulary, amount of dialogue,
number of characters, and approximate number of
words on each page.

There are a number of websites that can guide you
through the process of recognizing and selecting
suitable vocabulary for each grade level. For example,
toddlers use single-syllable words, while third graders
understand, and prefer to use, longer words. You can
learn more about vocabulary levels by doing a Google
search for *books by guided reading levels*. Also, seeking
guidance from a children's librarian or elementary
school media specialist is extremely helpful.

You are off to a good start.
Armed with a sound story idea, and having zeroed
in on your target audience, your job of crafting an
excellent children's book will become easier. Treat your
readers respectfully. Write only what you would want
to read.

*"The greatest part of a writer's time is
spent in reading, in order to write."*
                    —Samuel Johnson

PART 2

An Idea Takes Shape

5

Begin With an Idea

Every writing journey begins with an idea. Will your idea make a good story?

Is your idea a good one? How will you know?
The first people I share my ideas with are children. They are my valued critics. Kids are brutally honest and are not at all shy about telling you how they truly feel. I consider this a good thing because I want to hear the truth.

Listening to children's thoughts will often add to your own ideas and may help you develop a better story. Asking a simple question, such as, "What do you think the character should do next?" often leads to a major brainstorming session. Be sure to listen closely to what the children have to say. I have trashed a number of ideas that children did not like. (They hated my idea for The Button Fairy.) On the other hand, I have incorporated many ideas from children into my books: The Freckle Fairy concept was an idea from a child, and the illustrations for The Sock Fairy were planned with the assistance of a first grade class.

Unlike any other genre, children's books must also please the grownups; *they* will be the ones to purchase your book. One way to find out if they like your idea is to write a short description of your proposed story idea and read it to a few friends. It's wise to get their opinions *before* going through the trouble and expense of publishing. If adults don't like your idea, ask them why—and listen carefully to their replies. For example, if your idea is to write a story about a child who teaches his dog to sit under the table and wait for the scraps of food that the child doesn't like, that book may not be popular with adults.

Where will you find an idea?
Many of us have said, "That's a great idea—and so simple. Why didn't I think of that?" Look around you. Listen to what children are saying to each other as they play. If we could see ideas floating around like the thought bubbles in a book, the air would be filled with them. Topics as mundane as pumpkin pie, a TV that doesn't work, a bug under a magnifying glass, or a kid wearing a super hero T-shirt as he cuts the grass could be turned into a story. If you were to give these topics to a group of 4- to 8-year-olds, they would surely weave a few magical tales.

Will you be able to develop your idea into a full-fledged story?
Does your idea have enough depth and interest to fill a book? For example, you may have a cute idea about a spaceship landing in a swimming pool, but then what?

Is your idea timeless?
Twenty years from now, will children still understand and relate to your idea? Will it still matter? What about ten years from now? Five years? Next year? This is an important consideration. Topics that are popular today may not be popular tomorrow. A timeless idea is

one that will remain relevant over the years.

If the theme you've chosen is treated with true feeling and emotion, and if your characters seem real, you will increase the chances that your story will stand the test of time. One bit of good news for authors of children's books is that *fantasy* and *silliness* have genuine staying power. Just look at some of the books that have been around, and popular since the last century: *Winnie the Pooh, Charlotte's Web, Charlie and the Chocolate Factory,* and of course my all-time favorites, the Dr. Seuss books.

Is your idea popular, but not too popular?
It's always a surprise (and not a good one) to find out that your idea—the one that you were sure was the most original and exciting idea in the world—has been used before. If that's the case, it's best to find that out early in your journey.

You may have a decision to make: Shall I move on to a new idea, or are there ways that I can make my story different from all the others? Can I approach the idea from a new perspective, perhaps with a different narrator? Does this mean the market is saturated, or does it mean there's a huge audience waiting for me?

Do your homework. Find out what is actually selling and what is *not* selling. Visit your local library and bookstores, and check the many online resources. Read the top-selling children's books for your target age group. What are they about? What makes them special? Most importantly, how will *you* make *your* idea shine?

Test Your Idea

Here's one quick way to test your idea by using the basic information-gathering questions: **Who? What? Where? When? Why? How?**

Who will be my main character?
What issue will my story resolve?
Where will my story take place? (Indoors or outdoors? In a school? On a farm?)
When does my story take place? (What season or time of day?)
Why are my characters doing what they do? (This is called *character motivation.*)
How is the problem resolved or the lesson learned?

Using a theoretical example of an unhappy goldfish, let's see if we have enough of an idea to develop a story:
Who? Goldie the goldfish
What? A new fish is brought into her peaceful home. Goldie refuses to play with her.
Where? In her fishbowl
When? One bright afternoon
Why? Goldie doesn't want to share her space.
How? The two fish realize they both came from the same pet shop. Both love the cookie crumbs that the boy drops into their bowl. They realize how much they have in common, recognizing that friendship is a good thing.

Good news! The story idea above does seem to have enough things going for it to warrant continuing the story development. Now's the time to share the idea with a few children. I'll bet they will have a lot of ideas for filling in the details.

"Everybody walks past a thousand story ideas every day. The good writers are the ones who see five or six of them. Most people don't see any."

—*Orson Scott Card*

.

6

From an Idea
to an Outline

Once you have thought about your idea and answered the important questions—*Who? What? Where? When? Why? How?*—it's time to create an outline. It is more efficient to begin the actual writing process with an outline than to simply sit yourself down and write the entire story. Using an outline based on the three necessary parts of a story will enable you to sort your ideas and view the entire story at a glance.

Creating an outline is an important step that will help reveal areas of the story that may need more development. For example, if you have very little to say about one of the sections, it becomes obvious that this particular section needs to be strengthened.

Begin by dividing your outline into three sections that consist of the three main parts of a story.

> This is what your outline will look like:
> 1. Beginning
> 2. Middle
> 3. End

Next, using the goldfish idea in Chapter 5 as an example, add a few sentences under each heading, listing the main points and action of the story:

1. Beginning
  a. We meet Goldie the goldfish.
  b. She is happy.
  c. She has lots of room to swim and splash.
  d. One day a little boy drops another fish into Goldie's bowl.
  e. The boy calls the new fish Molly.

2. Middle
  a. Goldie is not happy.
  b. She doesn't like to share.
  c. The new fish wants to share Goldie's space and her food.
  d. Now the boy gives them more food—even cookie crumbs.
  e. They enjoy diving for cookie crumbs.
  f. Goldie likes Molly's long eyelashes.
  g. Goldie and Molly both like to sing and talk.
  h. They realize how much fun it is to race around the bowl.

3. End
  a. The two fish discover that they came from the same pet shop.
  b. They realize how much they have in common.
  c. They realize how good it feels to share.
  d. They recognize that they can be friends and that two can have more fun than one.

What you now have are the basic *bones* of the story. Now you can see your story at a glance. This was the easy part. All you need to do now is fill in with details, including action, narration and dialogue. That's a bit more difficult, but the process has begun.

Take a deep breath. I'll walk you through it...

"Begin at the beginning, and go on till you come to the end; then stop."

—Lewis Carroll

7

Story Structure and Arc: The Parts of a Story

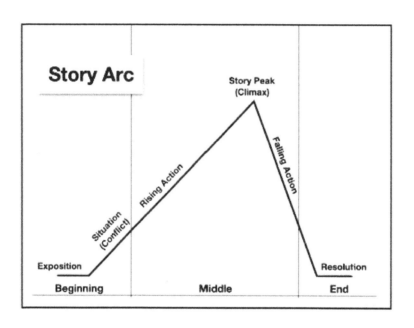

In literature, the term *structure* refers to the plot and framework of a story. Within this framework is the *story arc,* or *narrative arc,* which is the progression of the story. The three basic parts of a story *arc* are the beginning, middle and end. Within these three main sections are the *exposition, situation (conflict), rising action, story peak (climax), falling action* and *resolution.*

Beginning

The exposition establishes the start of the arc. This is where you set the scene and mood, introduce the main character (or characters), and lead into the conflict that will carry the characters through their journeys.

> **Examples:** The character can be happily setting out to find a new home, angrily trying to find the whereabouts of his missing bike, sadly saying goodbye to a brother who's leaving for college, or earnestly seeking a way to earn money.

This is where the reader learns the name, characteristics, and mindset of the main character. Even if this character is a car, a truck, a dog, or a bird, this information is necessary in order to build the foundation of the *plot*, or *sequence of events*. It is essential for the young reader to grasp this basic information in the beginning. Sometimes the secondary characters are also introduced in the beginning; other times, they appear later in the story.

Another important aspect of the story that we learn in the beginning is the setting, which is often revealed through the illustrations. Is the story taking place at home? In school? On a farm? In a spaceship?

Most importantly, the beginning is where the reader learns what the situation is that is causing a conflict for the main character. What is the problem the character is trying to solve? What is causing the conflict? Resolving this conflict will carry the main character through the story.

Middle

The middle is where you use the characters to develop the conflict. Throughout the middle, the *arc* of the character's journey is rising (progressing with tension). With this rising action, we follow the struggle, or the problem that needs to be resolved, as the characters head toward the peak of the arc (the climax). Throughout the middle, the main character should be moving toward solving this problem/conflict. For example, perhaps the main character is building a lemonade stand as a way to earn money, or trying to find a way to keep people from throwing plastic into the ocean.

The middle is where we see interactions with the other characters who help or hinder the main character's plans. This may include the neighborhood bully trying to keep the main character from building his lemonade stand, or children helping out by putting up signs to keep people from throwing plastic into the ocean.

As the characters set about to resolve the conflict, you must build tension and establish enough suspense to hold the readers' interest and drive the action forward. The reader needs to feel the tension mounting and anxiously anticipate what will happen next. How will the character open his lemonade stand when the bully keeps knocking it down? Will the new signs keep people from throwing plastic into the ocean, or do we also need more trash cans?

Most of the time, there are several attempts (often three, but not mandatory) by the character to solve the problem or reach the destination. With each attempt, the character shows a little more force and determination to move the story forward.

The most important part of the middle is the climax. We see one last push by the main character as he resolves the situation with a satisfying conclusion. This is where he finally finishes building his lemonade stand or putting up the newly-painted signs and trash cans to stop people from throwing plastic into the ocean. After the arc peaks (climax), it descends, creating the falling action and giving the reader the feeling that closure is drawing near.

End

Once your character succeeds, the story should head toward resolution and end as quickly and smoothly as possible. Don't drag it out! The lemonade stand is bringing in lots of money, and the fish can now swim without the danger of getting caught in the plastic.

The end is where we find out what the main character has learned—and it doesn't always have to be stated. When a situation is resolved, children learn the lesson right along with the characters. A good way to end a book is by tying it directly to the main point that was made in the beginning of the story. Our main character's goal is met as he is able to buy a new bike with the money he made selling lemonade. People are reading the signs and throwing plastic in trash cans instead of the ocean. With the conclusion of the characters' journey, the arc is complete.

In some fantasy books, there may be no real lesson learned. The end can simply accentuate the fun and happiness expressed throughout the book. This is similar to reading a happy poem with no real lesson, just a feel-good experience.

A quick three-part review

For a quick review, let's look at the popular book, *Charlie and the Chocolate Factory,* by Roald Dahl:

In the *beginning,* we meet Charlie and his family and learn that the situation involves finding a golden ticket and setting out—along with four other children—to compete for the big prize. The winner will tour the factory and receive a lifetime supply of chocolate.

In the *middle,* the *rising action* is felt as each child is put to a test, then ejected, one by one, from the factory for being greedy and obnoxious. We are now at the *climax.* Only Charlie remains.

At the *end,* the *falling action* is felt as the other contenders are gone and Charlie is now also being tested. The *resolution* is reached when Charlie learns that he has not only won the prize; the entire chocolate factory will one day belong to him!

Exceptions to the three-part structure

It's important to note that there are some books that do not have a three-part structure or a real plot. The following types of books do not fit this rule:

- Board books (or other toddler books)
- Alphabet books
- Books that express their message in list form, such as books about sea shells, fairies, dinosaurs, or types of trucks
- Non-fiction books such as travelogues or science books

Story arc division:

Knowing how many pages are needed for each part of the story is not an exact science; however, here is one *suggested guideline*:

The *beginning* takes place in the first 4 to 5 pages. The scene is set, the character and situation are described, and the arc begins. Then it is time to ramp up the action.

The *middle* takes 20 to 22 pages. The character and situation evolve, heading toward the peak of the arc. By the end of this section, the main character has resolved the situation.

The *end* takes place on the last 4 to 5 pages. The situation is resolved and the problem is resolved. The story and arc are complete.

"When you're telling a story, the best stories, every character has an arc. Every one. And that arc is usually about finding yourself, or about at least finding something about yourself that you didn't know."

—Roy Conli

Story Arc:
The path a
story follows

PART 3

The Language of Writing

8
The Basics of Writing a Sentence

The writing style needed to appeal to children is different from that of writing for adults. Just as you must match your topics and style of books to your audience, you must also match your words. When writing for young children, it's important to use clear, short sentences, rather than long, complex ones. This is especially true for the youngest readers, who are just learning to process written words. For many of these readers, concentrating on the letters is difficult enough, without having to keep track of a string of different thoughts.

Below is a brief *grammar refresher* that will also offer useful information to authors for whom English is not their first language. Here are some basic rules:

Simple sentence
Most children's books are written with *simple sentences*. A simple sentence expresses a complete thought and contains a *subject (noun)* and a *verb (predicate)*.

The *subject* is *who* or *what* the sentence is about.

Examples: dog, boy, dinosaur, bike, mom, dad, horse, cow, house, car, Billy, Sally

The *verb* describes what the subject is *doing or has already done.*

Examples: cry, bounce, run, ran, walk, walking, walked

The verb can also tell you the *condition of the subject* or their *state of being.*

Example: *Billy is happy.* The verb in this sentence is the word *is.*

Examples of simple sentences:
- The boy walks down the street. (*Boy* is the subject; *walks* is the verb.)
- The ball rolled away. (*Ball* is the subject; *rolled* is the verb.)
- Sally cried at school. (*Sally* is the subject; *cried* is the verb.)

To offer more information to the reader, you can add a descriptive word (adjective) to the subject:

Examples:
- The *red-headed* boy walks down the street.
- The *big red* ball rolled away.
- *Little* Sally cried at school.

You can also add a descriptive word (adverb) to the verb:

Examples:
- The red-headed boy walks *lazily* down the street.
- The big red ball *slowly* rolled away.
- Little Sally cried *loudly.*

You can change the tense, or time frame:

> **Present tense:** The red-headed boy *walks lazily* down the street.
> **Past tense:** The red-headed boy *walked lazily* down the street.

Compound sentence

A *compound sentence* is created when two or more *simple sentences* are attached to make one longer sentence. They are not simply stuck together; they must be connected with a word (conjunction) such as *for, and, but, or, yet, as, so.* A comma is normally used before the conjunction. (Simple sentences can also be attached with a semicolon; however, most children's authors prefer to use commas.)

Examples of compound sentences:
- The red-headed boy walked down the street, *but* he turned back when he reached the corner.
- The big red ball is rolling away, *and* I hope I will be able to catch it.
- Why is little Sally crying loudly, *yet* everyone else is smiling?

Appropriate sentences for different age groups

The type and length of sentences you use need to be written specifically for the age group you are targeting and the type of book you are writing.

Board books

Typically, these books contain from zero to three words per page and are written for toddler and preschool children. Simple words, such as *ball* or *big ball,* are all that are needed. If sentences are used, they are very short, such as *See the ball.*

Picture books

Most picture books are geared to children ages 4 to 8. Keep in mind that children in this age group typically have short attention spans. Picture books should contain *simple sentences* that are enhanced by the use of adjectives and adverbs. Young readers grasp the meaning of words more easily if the sentences are short and deal with one thought at a time. You can still add a few compound sentences if you feel they are needed, however be sure to keep their meaning simple enough for the younger members of your audience to understand.

Other types of children's books

For children who have outgrown picture books and moved on to chapter books, it is preferable to use compound sentences. Many teachers prefer longer sentences at this level because more detail can be included. Additionally, older children find that longer sentences sound more *grown up*—and more like the way we actually speak. Middle grade books use adult-like language.

Punctuation dos and don'ts

For the most part, your editor will correct your punctuation; however, there are a few *dos and don'ts* to keep in mind while writing your story:

- Do put a period at the end of each sentence—even in a rhyming story and in dialogue.
- Do put quotation marks before and after the actual words your characters are saying—even in a rhyming story.
- Do capitalize the first word in a sentence.
- Don't overuse exclamation marks. Try using a more emphatic descriptive word instead.

Examples:
- **Before:** *Mom, I'm tired!*
  After: *Mom, I'm exhausted.*
- **Before:** *That elephant is big!*
  After: *That elephant is enormous.*

Don't overuse any one punctuation mark. More is not better; too much punctuation can cause clutter and confusion.

"If you bring that sentence in for a fitting, I can have it shortened by Wednesday."
—Hawkeye, a character in M.A.S.H.

9

Tone and Vocabulary: Feelings and Words

Children's books, especially *picture books*, offer less space for story development than books for older children and young adults. For this reason, the language is extremely important to the story. If you choose your words carefully and keep your target audience in mind, you can create a story that children will want to hear over and over again.

Tone

Set the tone.
It's not only the words that matter in a story or conversation; it's also the *tone* with which the words are spoken. A story's tone is set by the language and actions of the main character or narrator, and helps form the connection to your readers' emotions and feelings. The more you can relate to your readers, the stronger their engagement with your story will be. Through the use of words, tone reflects the mood or attitude of your story. I believe that everyone, at some point, has either said or been told, "Don't use that tone with me." Or as my mother always said, "It's not what you say that matters; it's the way that you say it." This is an important concept to keep in mind when writing for children. For picture book readers, characters should not

be combative. They can disagree, be angry about something, or feel sad, but not to the point of rudeness or aggressiveness. Through your characters, you must realize that *you* are talking to the reader. What is the feeling you wish your story to convey?

The best way to know how your story *feels* is to have someone read it aloud to you. If your characters are *shouting, shrieking* or *boasting* all the time, you should probably choose calmer language to describe their actions.

"Voices have a language of their own and communicate much more than the words that they say." —Indu Muralidharan

Vocabulary

Use appropriate vocabulary.
Simply put, the term *vocabulary* refers to the words needed to communicate effectively. Vocabulary creates the basis for reading comprehension; therefore, it's crucial for you to be familiar with the vocabulary of your target age group in order to make the meaning of your story clear and understandable. In most cases, it's fine to introduce children to a few new words, but only if these words are used correctly and in sentences in which their meaning is clear.

One way to introduce a new word is to let one of the characters use the word and then have them follow up by offering the definition.

Example: Let's use the word *dilapidated*.
If a character says, "Look at that *dilapidated* house," a young reader may not know the meaning of the word. But by adding further dialogue, the character can then explain the meaning to another character by saying, "It hasn't been taken care of and it looks like it's about to fall down."

Another way to introduce a new word is to use it in a sentence in a way that will illustrate the meaning of the word:

Example: Let's use the word *impressed*.
Context clues can provide a useful tool for teaching new vocabulary words. When used in context, the word *impressed* is easily understood. If a young character in a story is told by a parent or teacher, "I'm very *impressed* with the good work you've done," the definition of *impressed* is made clear without an actual explanation, especially when coupled with an illustration of that smiling, proud adult.

Choose new words carefully.
Adding bigger words to a story can help build the readers' vocabulary, but it's important to choose the words carefully. For example, if you are writing for the 4 to 8 age group, adding words that are understandable to most 8-year-olds can help build the vocabulary of the lower end of the age group. But if you add words that typically appear on the vocabulary lists of most 12-year-olds, your younger readers may not be able to understand the story. For guidance, you can Google *vocabulary lists* for each grade.

What you don't want to do is randomly sprinkle unknown words throughout your story in the hopes that the grownup who may be reading the book to a child will take the time to stop and explain each word. Even if this *were* to happen, it would create a number of stumbling blocks to the flow of the story. For the most part, it's best to use language that will be understood by your target audience.

Is there a place for slang?
Slang is simply the use of informal language; it exists in every culture and in every spoken language. Slang words often come from the lazy mispronunciation of words and phrases that eventually become a part of everyday vocabulary. Is there a place for slang in children's books? While some readers and writers feel that using slang is appropriate, others believe that it limits the reading audience.

Slang words include everything from *ain't, gotcha* and *cool* to the more recent terms such as *dope, yo* and *rad.*

If you want your book to appeal to a wide audience, you need to face the reality that the use of slang may be off-putting to some people. However, when writing for teens, slang often becomes a more normal way of speaking, and without it the story may not be as effective. Be careful. Do your research and be sure the words you are using will not be offensive to people of any culture.

Another consideration when using slang: If you plan to translate your book to another language, you may face a challenge.

Add a few quirky or made-up words.
While not exactly *normal* vocabulary words, there are many quirky and made-up words that are fun to read. Scattered throughout a story, they add a bit of silliness that kids love. Keep in mind that if you are planning to have your book translated into different languages, just as with slang, these words will be difficult to translate.

Examples:

bamboozle	helter-skelter
cowabunga	hurly-burly
diddly-squat	jibber-jabber
doohickey	lollapalooza
fuddy-duddy	shenanigans
gizmo	thingamajig
gobbledygook	topsy-turvy

"Don't use a five-dollar word when a fifty-cent word will do."

—Mark Twain

10
Create Colorful Imagery: Adjectives and Verbs

Have you ever thought of words as colorful? Some words actually create colorful images in the mind of the reader and can help turn a mediocre story into a bestseller.

The Use of Adjectives

Adjectives are descriptive words that create imagery, or *thought pictures*, in the readers' minds. They are one of the most useful and important parts of the language in children's books. Adjectives awaken children's senses, inviting them into a more enjoyable experience.

The basic use of adjectives is to *describe*; adjectives add information to the way something looks, sounds, tastes, feels, or smells.

Before and after examples:

- a pile of mud —> a pile of **slimy** mud
- the boy —> the **red-headed** boy
- the noise —> the **thundering** noise
- the chick —> the **fuzzy, yellow** chick
- Mom's brownies —> Mom's **fudgy** brownies

The overuse of adjectives

If one adjective is good, then more adjectives are better, right? Sorry, wrong. Adjectives should not be used in excess. Save the use of an occasional string of adjectives to describe a main character, but don't overload too many of your words with an abundance of adjectives. Overuse can make the story feel tedious and weighted down. Remember, your illustrations will be showing the things you are describing, so you can eliminate extra words by not stating too much of the obvious. *Less is more*; one well-chosen adjective will usually get your point across.

Example of excessive adjectives:
The sweet, little, yellow, fuzzy chick was going for a much-needed long walk when she fell in a big, slippery, slimy mud puddle.

A string of adjectives

Be concise. Avoid using a string of adjectives that have the same meaning. If an adjective is not adding information, don't use it. In each of the examples below, any one of the adjectives will suffice; using them all together is redundant.

Examples:
- It was a *shiny, bright, sunny* day.
- She was a *smiling, happy* pup.
- Mom's lap was *soft, cuddly, cozy* and *warm*

Overuse of the words *very* and *really*

If you choose your adjectives correctly, you will be able to avoid the two words that many of us have come to rely on: *very* and *really*.

The problem is that these words are overused to the point of no longer being effective. There are many adjectives to choose from instead, and the result is a stronger sentence.

Before and after examples:

Very:
- a **very** small cat —> a **teensy** kitty
- a **very** happy child —> a **fun-loving** child
- a **very** big elephant —> a **ginormous** elephant
- a **very** bright light —> a **brilliant** light

Really:
- a **really** pretty dress —> a **gorgeous** dress
- a **really** bright moon —> a **dazzling** moon
- a **really** smart girl —> a **genius**
- a **really** smelly odor —> a **stinky** smell

My advice is to avoid the use of *very* and *really* whenever possible.

The Use of Verbs

Verbs are words that express action. Like adjectives, they play an important role in children's books and also create colorful imagery. Everything a character does is an action: run, walk, talk, think, play, etc. When writing a story, it helps to think of verbs as either *weak* or *strong*.

Weak verbs
A weak verb is not a *wrong* verb; the term *weak* refers to a *basic* verb.
Examples: *got, went, is, moved, said, put.*
These words are boring and ineffective and should be replaced with stronger verbs.

Strong verbs
A *strong* verb is a more descriptive version of a verb. It conjures up a more exciting image of what the character is doing and helps you get your point across.

Converting a weak verb to a strong verb:
· The horse **moved** to the pasture. —>
· The horse **galloped** to the pasture.

· Dylan **walked** to the playground. —>
· Dylan **darted** to the playground.

· She **got** all the plates from the table. —>
· She **gathered** all the plates from the table.

· Ellie **talks** all day. —>
· Ellie **chatters** all day.

· The deer **ate** the carrot. —>
· The deer **chomped** the carrot.

· Danny **drank** his milk quickly. —>
· Danny **guzzled** his milk.

· The dog **went** after the bone. —>
· The dog **pounced** on the bone.

One action-packed verb can eliminate a lot of unneeded words from your story. The Merriam-Webster Dictionary defines action-packed as *filled with action...and excitement*. These are things that children thrive on. Using them in your writing will help make your story come alive. But choose your verbs wisely—and frugally. An online **thesaurus** is the perfect tool to guide you. As with adjectives, avoid the overuse of strong verbs. Too many characters darting, chattering and gliding around can overpower a story.

Substitute 'damn' every time you're inclined to write 'very;' your editor will delete it and the writing will be just as it should be."

—Mark Twain

11

Elements of Language That Children Like Best

There are some elements of language that work particularly well in children's books. Sprinkling these elements throughout your story can enliven the story and offer your readers words that are fun to read over and over again. The impact of your words can hold the key to unlocking your story.

Hyperbole
Hyperbole is the use of extreme exaggeration, often to the point of being hilarious. Ideas and thoughts that are expressed using hyperbole may seem ridiculous—or downright impossible—but that's the point. Hyperboles are not meant to be taken literally, and are often so extreme that even the more literal-minded children know they are not real. This is a useful tool for delivering a message in a way that children will remember. It's even possible to create an entire story based on exaggeration. Tall tales are perfect examples of hyperbole, with books about Paul Bunyan and Johnny Appleseed remaining popular for decades.

Why not give your character a unique ability? Stretch your imagination. Reach for the stars!

Examples of *hyperbole*:
- The cow jumped over the moon.
- My backpack weighs a ton.
- Our new car cost a gazillion dollars.
- I've already read that book a million times.
- Johnny can run as fast as the wind.
- I'm baking the biggest cookie in the world.
- My Dad snores louder than a freight train.
- I've told you a thousand times not to do that.

Personification

Personification is giving an animal or inanimate object a quality or ability that is normally attributed to a human. In children's stories, this tool can add a new element, enabling you to bring non-human things to life. Even if your character is a truck, you can give it human qualities that will allow young readers to react to it emotionally.

A familiar example of *personification*:
Hey, diddle, diddle,
The cat and the fiddle,
The cow jumped over the moon;
The little dog laughed
To see such sport,
And the dish ran away with the spoon.

Other examples of personification:
- Tillie the truck was sad to be out in the rain.
- The garden was begging for water.
- The wind howled like a wolf.
- My alarm clock screamed at me to wake up.

Sound Devices

Sound devices can be used to draw attention to words you wish to emphasize, or to create a special mood.

Onomatopoeia
Always a favorite sound device with young readers, *onomatopoeia* is when words are used to imitate actual sounds. This is an area where you can even make up your own words and get away with it. Children love to read *onomatopoeic words* out loud. The words are often printed in capital letters for emphasis.

Examples of *onomatopoeia*:
> SPLASH! GURGLE! SWOOSH! WOOF!
> DING DONG! TICK TOCK! BOOM! ARF!
> GROWL! ROAR! NEIGH!

Examples of using onomatopoeia to turn a simple sentence into a fun experience:

- Jamie turned the faucet on. —>
- SPLASH! There was water all over the place.

- Fluffy barked to go outside. —>
- WOOF, WOOF! Fluffy barked excitedly.

- I hope I'm not late for school. —>
- Jimmy hurried. TICK TOCK! Will he make it on time?

Alliteration

Alliteration refers to a series of words or sentences that begin with the same sound, most often a consonant sound. There are other types of *alliteration*, but initial consonant alliteration is the most popular in children's books. This repetition adds an enticing rhythm and makes a phrase easy to read and fun to say out loud. Remember that the consonant *sound* must be the same, not just the initial letter. For example, **Ch**eerful **Ch**arlie is alliterative, but **C**areful **Ch**arlie is not.

Giving your main characters an alliterative name can make them more interesting—and more memorable. Think of Mickey Mouse, Donald Duck and Spongebob Squarepants. But don't go overboard. Too many *alliterations* can be *too terrifically and terribly tongue-tying.*

More examples of alliteration:
- Billy was busy as a bee.
- Silly Sally salamander sat in the sun.
- Callie made cookies, candy and cupcakes galore.
- Lizzy the lizard now learned how to leap.
- The bug was a bully and bit the beetle.

Tongue-twisters are also examples of alliteration:
- Peter Piper picked a peck of pickled peppers.
- The big black bug bit a big black bear.
- Sherry sheared the shabby sheep.

Repetition

When practicing any skill, the more one rehearses, the easier the skill becomes. It's the same with reading, which is why repetition is a widely used feature of children's books. Repeating the same words reinforces children's memory skills and can also help the writer emphasize a point. The grammatical pattern of repetition adds rhythm to the text, helping young readers remember what they have read.

Be sure you choose important words that are worth repeating and, as with other elements of language, be careful not to overdo it.

Repetition can be used in both rhyme and prose and can be effectively used with phrases or individual words. The words or phrases you choose should be repeated within close proximity of each other.

Example of using a repetitive phrase in a story:
A child looking for a missing shoe can ask over and over again, "Where IS that shoe? Where IS that shoe?" Then each time he comes close to finding it, he can say, "Nope, THAT'S not my shoe." In this case, both sentences are repeated.

Examples of repetition:
- Over and over and over again.
- Up, up, up he flew.
- Let it snow, let it snow, let it snow.
- Row, row, row, your boat.

A popular book that uses repetition very successfully is *Five Little Monkeys* by Eileen Christelow.

Before and After: Add Some Fun

The before and after versions of the following paragraph illustrate the impact that the elements of language described in this chapter can have on your story:

Before: Betty skipped to school. She was in kindergarten. Suddenly she saw a big mud puddle. "It must have rained last night," she said.

After: Betty the Bunny was bippity-bopping along to school when she saw something up ahead. It was the biggest squishy-squashy mud puddle in the world! Betty bippity-bopped right into the puddle. SQUISH! STOMP! SPLASH!

When words are fun, reading becomes fun—and creating colorful language should be high on your list of goals when writing for children.

"The limits of my language mean the limits of my world."
—Ludwig Wittgenstein

Sprinkle your stories with fun.

12

Be Careful with Figures of Speech

Figures of speech are phrases that can be used for effect; they can elevate words beyond their literal meaning. If used correctly, figures of speech can embellish a story; but if overused, or used incorrectly, they can turn a story into a disaster. It's important to understand what *figures of speech* are, and which ones are understandable to each age group.

Simile

A *simile* uses the words *like* or *as* to compare two things. This is a figure of speech that even young children are able to understand, especially when paired with an illustration. One effective way to demonstrate the meaning of a simile is through the use of an illustrated thought bubble over the character's head as he imagines himself as a lion or a frog, etc. Similes work well in picture books.

Examples of similes:
- brave as a lion
- quiet as a mouse
- angry as a bear
- flat as a pancake
- funny as a barrel of monkeys
- clean as a whistle
- jumpy like a frog
- squiggly like a worm
- soared like an eagle

Metaphor

A *metaphor* makes an indirect comparison between two things that are not actually alike. In other words, the comparison is not literally true. For the youngest readers, who tend to be very literal, metaphors can be confusing and are generally not suitable. For example, if you say, "She had a broken heart," you can just imagine what horrors might go through the mind of a 3- or 4-year old. If your target audience is middle grade and above, they will be more likely to understand and appreciate metaphors.

Examples of metaphors:
- We are in the same boat.
- His cheeks were on fire.
- He's a couch potato.
- My sister is a night owl.
- He's just a chicken.
- The class was a zoo.
- Life is a rollercoaster.

Idiom

Idioms are phrases that have become common sayings and are not meant to be taken literally—and that's precisely the problem when using them in children's books. Most of the time, young readers just don't *get it*. Middle grade children understand and appreciate idioms.

One problem you might run into with idioms is that their meaning hardly ever translates well into other languages.

Examples of idioms:
- Don't bang your head against the wall.
- Are you getting cold feet?
- That's a piece of cake.
- It's raining cats and dogs.
- I have a frog in my throat.
- Stop pulling my leg.
- He looked at her and drew a blank.
- She gave it a shot.

Cliche

A *cliche* is a phrase or opinion that is overused...and overused...to the point of becoming trite. And if that isn't enough reason to avoid the use of cliches, think of this: Young readers will likely have no clue what you are talking about. Actually, many cliches are unclear even to adults. As you read the list below, remember that young minds will take these literally. Middle grade children and above are generally able to figure out the meaning of *cliches*, even if they haven't heard them before.

Examples of cliches:
- She's as pretty as a picture.
- He had his tail between his legs.
- Laughter is the best medicine.
- He was scared out of his wits.
- She could see the writing on the wall.
- His mind wandered.
- That really takes the cake.

Figures of speech can enhance—or destroy—a story. If you choose to use them, be sure you know and understand the comprehension level of your intended audience.

13

Don't Fall in Love
With Your Words

One of the best pieces of advice I can give to all aspiring writers is: Don't fall in love with your words!

A story can often benefit from the replacement of one word with a more suitable word; or sometimes a story simply has too many words. Either way, it's wise to keep an open mind. If a professional editor recommends that you remove some of your words, my advice is to *let the words go.* If the recommendation is that you choose a different word, be flexible. Remember that there are still hundreds of thousands of perfectly good words left to choose from.

Is the word count too high for the type of book you are writing?
If you are planning to submit your manuscript to a traditional publisher, you must first ask what their guidelines are regarding word count. If you choose not to follow their guidelines, your manuscript will not be considered—no matter how beautiful your words may be.

If you are planning to self-publish, you should still adhere to the recommended word count. The established suggestions are based on both traditional and current educational guidelines. (See Chapter 3: *Types of Children's* Books.)

Perfect word count is not the only consideration.
In children's books, every word must count. But even if your word count is perfect, you may still have words that do not enhance your story. If that's the case, eliminate them—even if you love them.

Read each of your sentences and ask yourself: Does this line contribute anything to my story? Will the story still make sense without these words? When your story is ready to be edited, it may be time to end this part of your relationship with some of your words.

Avoid padded language.
Padded language refers to the use of more words than are necessary to express a thought or idea. Sometimes authors are tempted to add needless or repetitive information to the story for the purpose of meeting their projected word count. To young readers, the use of too many words creates a distraction from the plot and forward movement of the story. Remember: Write only what you need. (Also see Chapter 10: *Create Colorful Imagery: Adjectives and Verbs.)*

Here's an example of an *extremely* padded sentence:

Even though it was very and totally unnecessary for the shaggy, poodle-like young puppy to walk slowly down the skinny, narrow path in the very cold snow, he certainly and deliberately managed to do this, making sure that he didn't slide on the cold, wet ice that was under his feet the whole entire time.

The following list offers suggestions for removing padded language:

Instead of:	Try this:
at the end of	after
at the present moment	now
is located in	is in
rarely ever	rarely
due to the fact that	because
what I want is	I want
which was when	when
in view of the fact that	because
managed to do it	did it

Be wary of dead words.
After you say goodbye to the unnecessary words, be on the lookout for the *dead words* that might be clogging your story.

Words that are frequently overused and do not add meaning to a story are often referred to as *dead words*. Due to overuse, they have lost their power and turned to clutter. Your sentences will be more meaningful and more *alive* without these words.

Examples of dead words:
really, got, nice, pretty, then, very, a lot, good, fun

Instead of:	Try this:
I had a **really** good time.	I had a **fabulous** time.
He **got** a big gift.	He **received** a big gift.
The new girl is **nice**.	The new girl is **friendly**.
That's **pretty** bad.	That's **dreadful.**
If you yell, **then** I will cry.	If you yell, I will cry.
The puppy is **very** cute.	The puppy is **adorable**.
He tattles **a lot**.	He **often** tattles.
You did a **good** job.	You did an **excellent** job.
That was **fun**.	That was **enjoyable**.

Here is a *before and after* example of how to remove dead, meaningless words from a story:

Before:

The sun is shining brightly.

"Good morning," says Dad. "It's really time to wake up, sleepyhead."

"Good morning, Dad," Andrea mumbles sleepily. She gives a very big yawn.

"Hurry and get dressed. We have to pick up Grandma to go to the fair," Dad says.

"Come on, sleepyhead," says Mom, as she peeks in through the door. Breakfast is ready."

Andrea slides out of bed, then throws on her clothes and runs to the bathroom to brush her teeth. Then she scurries downstairs. **(83 words)**

After:
"Wake up, sleepyhead!" shouts Dad. "Today's the day we are going to the fair. Grandma is waiting and breakfast is ready, so I'll see you in the kitchen in 10 minutes. Ready...set...go!" **(34 words)**

In the **before** example above, the reader does not need to be told that the sun is shining or that Mom is peeking in the bedroom door; the illustrations can take care of that. Other bits of information such as yawning, brushing teeth and getting dressed do not add anything to the story. There are also a few dead words sprinkled into the mix. The **after** version gets the message across and is tighter and more exciting.

Avoid redundant expressions.
This means avoiding words that express the same meaning twice. If you can say it in one word, you don't need to use two.

Examples of redundant words:

- join together
- same identical
- end result
- exact same
- sit down

- new innovation
- share together
- return back
- unexpected surprise
- stand up

Reminder: Don't fall in love with your words. More is not better!

So the writer who breeds more words than he needs is making a chore for the reader who reads."

—Dr. Seuss

14

Be Succinct

The legend of Ernest Hemingway's 6-word story
Supposedly, sometime in the 1920s, Ernest Hemingway made a 10-dollar bet with a few other authors that he could write the shortest novel. Upon writing his now-famous 6-word story on a napkin, Hemingway won the bet. Although there is some doubt in the literary community that this actually occurred, it remains a perfect example of the art of writing succinctly, saying as much as you can in as few words as possible. It also demonstrates the fact that memorable story ideas can be found anywhere.

Here is Hemingway's story in its entirety:

For sale, Baby shoes, Never worn.

Remember this lesson as you write your book:
Be succinct!

Simplicity is the ultimate sophistication.
—Leonardo da Vinci

PART 4

Necessary
Story Elements

15

Write an Inviting Opening

Have you ever flipped through the TV channels, stopped to watch the beginning of a show, then moved on until something else piqued your interest? If so, you can identify with the dismay of a young reader who flips to the first page of a book and finds the initial paragraph too boring to continue. Children want to be entertained. This is why it is of utmost importance to let your readers know immediately that enjoyment is what you are offering.

Begin a sentence with, "Hey kids, listen to this!" or "You won't believe this!" and you will catch their attention. Your opening sentence is this type of invitation to the reader. Think about this as you write this important sentence. Your goal is to make your audience eager to keep reading, and to do so, you must create your own up-to-date, inviting opening and avoid the traditional *once upon a time*. Remember—you only get to make a first impression once.

Here are some suggestions and examples to guide you:

Begin quickly.
Make something happen right away. With children's books, the importance of making every word count is especially relevant when writing the first few sentences.

Capture your readers' attention quickly; then run with them—right into the story. You want your readers to wonder what will happen next. After the first sentence, quickly follow up with details that heighten the excitement of the opening.

Types of opening sentences:

An exciting statement.
- This was the best surprise ever!
- I am unstoppable!
- It was the biggest spider I ever saw!
- There's a strange creature living in our tree!

An intriguing question.
- Why is there snow inside the house?
- What are those mysterious black footprints?
- What is that silly snail up to now?
- How do you catch an octopus?

An action.
- Jimmy screamed and jumped up and down.
- Zoey couldn't stop laughing.
- The water splashed all over the place.
- The ostrich is running in circles again.

Meaningful dialogue.
- "I'm taking my turtle to school today, Mom."
- "I dreamed I was riding a crocodile."
- "Dad, my tooth is falling out!"
- "Dylan, give it back!"
- "Yikes! A monster ate my homework!"

You can even begin with a rhyme.
You can open a story with a teasing rhyme—even if
your story is not written in rhyme. A short, catchy
rhyme can be a fun way to begin, even for a story
written in prose.

> A robot ate my broccoli,
> and my carrots and my peas.
> Yes, this robot ate my broccoli,
> and he never once said please.

Rhyming books also need inviting openings.
If your story is written in rhyme, that doesn't let you
off the hook. Your story will still need a beginning,
middle and end, and you will still need to draw readers
into your story with an enticing opening.

**Examples of rhyming openings that will likely
pique the readers' interest:**

> Long, long ago and far, far away,
> Two robots came to town one day.
>
> .....
>
> I wish I were a creature, a hairy kind of guy,
> A hurly burly creature who only has one eye.
>
> .....
>
> I think I heard a funny sound.
> Did you hear it too?
> Perhaps a fairy made that sound.
> It couldn't have been you!

When NOT to add excitement to a story opening. There are exceptions to every rule. There are actually times when you do NOT want to offer a blast of excitement to a young reader; often a blanket of calmness is needed instead.

In a bedtime story or rhyming lullaby, it's important to set a quiet tone in the beginning and maintain it throughout the book. If you are writing a book for children who experience anxiety, calmness is the key. If you are writing a legend about a culture whose message is peace and love, such as many Native American legends, calmness is also the key. It's always imperative to know your audience.

Examples of calming opening sentences:
- The stars twinkle in the sky.
- As the sun sets over the small village, everyone gets ready for bed.
- The moon lights their way in the dark.
- I love you more than anything.

Once you are comfortable with your opening, work on maintaining a steady pace throughout the story. Always think in terms of *forward movement*.

"The most difficult thing about writing is writing the first line."
—Amit Kalantri

16

Create Compelling Characters

The characters you create have the important job of enacting your story and carrying it forward. Your task is to create strong characters that children will relate to and care about. This will give the story *staying power* and enable it to hold the interest of young readers from beginning to end.

Unlike adult books that normally involve a larger cast of characters, children's books need only the characters that play an important role in the life of the main character. The illustrations can be utilized if there is a place in the story where you wish to show a crowd on the playground or a busy classroom; however, young readers often find it difficult to keep track of more than a few named characters.

Create a Unique Main Character

The main character plays the most important role in the development of your story; therefore, this character should be developed first. It is imperative for you to know this character through and through.

The first step in character development is to picture the character in your mind. Then, with pencil and paper, allow your character to become real. Even if you are only able to draw stick figures, sketch what you are imagining. Add clothes, shoes, and maybe a hat. And don't forget the perfect hairdo. Write the character's name above the picture you have created.

> **Note:** Having the internet at your fingertips can help you with your sketch. For example, I was able to look at hundreds of *old lady clipart hairdos* before finding just the right one for my elderly Belly Button Fairy.

Make your main character memorable.
You have the power to create a character that will take on a life of its own. What will you do to make your main character memorable? Think of the most famous characters in children's books: Winnie-the-Pooh, Peter Pan, Pinocchio, Charlie in Willy Wonka, Alice, Matilda, etc. Remember: Each of them began just as you are beginning—with an idea and a character sketch.

Decide on the main character's personality and point of view.
As you begin the process of creating your main character, you will need to be mindful of:

- the personality you assign to this character.
- the manner in which this character will interact with the other characters.
- the way this character will be perceived by your target audience.

Only when you know your character inside and out, and understand how he will react in different situations, can you guide him through the story. (This part is often a little easier if you are used to interacting with children.)

Make a list of the character's personality traits, likes and dislikes. Is your character a silly kid who finds humor in everything? A carefree, boisterous, type? Very serious and studious? Or maybe very bashful? Describe how your character gets along with his siblings and/or classmates. Name his favorite pastimes. What does he like to wear? What is his favorite food? Is he a sleepyhead? Does he have a lot of friends? Is he cheerful? Is he gloomy?

Keep in mind that the character's point of view can change throughout the story as he learns a lesson or realizes he has made a mistake.

> **Example:** A character may start out being mopey and sad; he frowns and pouts because he is unable to ride his bike without training wheels. When he finally succeeds, he feels a sense of accomplishment that completely changes his attitude.

Don't divulge the character's age.
Even though *you* will know your character's age, it's usually not advisable to mention it in a story. The reason is that, once you mention the age or grade level of your characters, you have put a stamp on them.

Children even slightly older than the character will often see the book as *too babyfied*—even if the story and vocabulary are a fit for their actual reading skills. Conversely, children younger than the character may feel that the book will be too difficult for them.

When illustrating a children's book, it's a good idea to have the children in the story *look* just a bit older than the children in the age group you are targeting. Children identify with, and look up to, older children, and often shy away from books that picture children younger than themselves.

Disclaimer: This is usually *not* the case when writing for toddlers; they love illustrations of babies and other toddlers.

How Will Your Readers Perceive Your Main Character?

Even though you, as the author, must know everything about your main character, remember that children's books need to tell their story in as few words as possible. For this reason, you will need to keep your descriptions within the story to a minimum. The readers will learn about the character through dialogue, narration, and actions as the story plays out. (More to come in the next few chapters...)

Instead of describing your character with endless strings of adjectives, *show* his likes, dislikes, physical features, and attitude by tightening the language and expressing the information in just a few choice words—aided by the illustrations and dialogue. Choose an illustrator who is adept at creating different moods by changing body language and facial expressions.

Add the subtle use of props.
I've always been a fan of props. What characters carry
with them, or have lying around, can say a lot about
their personality—without the use of a single word.
Whether it's a book, a purse, a backpack, a baseball
cap, a teddy bear, or a skateboard, a prop not only
helps define a character's personality; it also adds
excitement and gives the reader something to search
for on each page.

If your main character is an animal, the prop might
be a bone, a sock monkey, or anything amusing
that relates to the character. These become items of
interest as they appear in different places throughout
the book.

Using my own books as examples, the Knot Fairy
carries a lantern and a book titled *How to Tie Knots in
Hair;* the Sock Fairy carries a wand and a flashlight;
the Belly Button Fairy carries a ruler and a bucket of
fairy dust; the Freckle Fairy carries night goggles and
a bag of supplies; the Fart Fairy always has his bag of
beans and a book titled *It Wasn't Me!*

Should You Base a Character on Someone You Know?

It can be extremely helpful to draw inspiration from
the children—or animals—in your life. Assigning
human qualities to the animals will, in most cases,
actually help make the characters more believable.
After all, most of what we know about different
personalities, such as shyness or quirkiness, comes
from people we have known.

There is a possible challenge that may arise if you try to base a character on someone you know too well— perhaps your own child. The challenge comes with wanting the character to be *exactly* like the child. For example, if your child is extremely shy and you place him in a story situation where he is playing a dominant role, you may need to make his dialogue stronger than his actual personality allows. If you choose to stay true to your child's personality, the story may suffer.

Many writers feel that if the *real* character wouldn't act a certain way, then the story character shouldn't act that way either. The conundrum is that you are writing a work of fiction. If the personality of the child meshes with the situation and allows you to showcase the theme, this is fine, but if you want to appeal to a broad audience, it's best to be flexible and make your characters fit the story.

A Main Character Can Be an Animal...or a Truck...or a Bug!

How wonderful it is to be able to create a truly original main character! In children's literature, it's perfectly normal for cars to talk, bees to sing in a band, fairies to come and visit, or bunnies to ride bikes. The main character can be a tree, a trolley, or even a rock! The right description, along with a talented illustrator, will even be able to give a bulldozer the right personality.

This concept can play out in one of two ways:

(1) The main character is an animal (or even an inanimate object), but there are humans in the story who facilitate the action. For example, in a story about a service dog, the owner may be the one guiding the dog's training throughout the plot. In this case, there are two main characters to develop, each with their own distinctive traits.

(2) In other stories, the dog (or car, or firefly) has human characteristics and carries the plot by interacting with other dogs, cars, or fireflies. In this case, you will create your main character in the same way that you would create a human character.

Create the Supporting Cast: The Other Characters

Creating the *supporting cast* is slightly less daunting than creating the main character. You still need to know who they are and what they look like, but instead of knowing these characters in great depth, their most important role will be the way they interact with the main character. For example, we don't need to know everything there is to know about the boy next door; all we are concerned with is the fact that he and our main character both climbed to the top of the jungle gym. For the main character, this may be an end to his fear of heights, but as far as the secondary character is concerned, we don't always need his background information.

Name your characters.
Choosing a character's name is often a sticking point for writers. I always suggest looking at the many online lists of baby names; there's a great chance that the perfect name will pop up.

Here are a few things to consider when naming your characters:

- **A name can have a hidden meaning.**
It's a good idea to Google a name before you give it to your character to be sure there is no negative meaning attached to it that would offend any culture or religion. If your book is about a specific culture, be sure to do your research to avoid choosing an inappropriate name.

- **A name can be difficult to pronounce.**
If you are writing for young children who are starting to read on their own, they may have difficulty pronouncing some names. This may mean avoiding names like Xiomara, Schuyler and Joaquin.

- **A name can be too long.**
Another element to consider when naming your character is the length of the name. If you have a character named Dingle Dot Dewberry Duck, it may sound cute once or twice, but it can become tedious after a few pages.

Don't make your characters stereotypical.
The days of the stereotypical family consisting of a
mother, father, son and daughter are no longer a
reality. If we embrace the different types of families
and relationships, and write about real-life issues
using non-stereotypical characters, we can educate our
readers.

>   **For example:**
>   • A lost billygoat can be raised by raccoons.
>   • A bully can be the smallest kid in the class.
>   • A fierce dog with huge teeth can be afraid
>   of a bug.
>   • A family can have two moms or two dads.
>   • A family can be racially mixed.

Make your characters all-inclusive.
The world we live in is an ever-evolving mosaic of
people with different backgrounds. For this reason, it
is important to include children of different ethnicities
and abilities in your stories whenever possible. This
will expand your audience and make your characters
more relatable. A perfect goal would be to have
children *everywhere* feel welcome when they open
your book.

*"It's relatively easy to create an ambiguous
character. Getting an audience to deeply
identify with a character, on the other
hand, is one of the hardest things in the
world to do."*

— Matt Bird

17
Every Story Needs a Narrator

Every written story is being told by someone. That *someone* is the narrator.

The role of the narrator
The *narrator* determines the story's point of view. When a child tells you about his day in school, he is using a *narrative* and telling you his version of a story. He is the narrator.

There are three different points of view, or narratives, to choose from when writing a children's story, and you will need to choose your path when you begin the process.

For the most part, it's important to keep the same narrator throughout the entire book. In adult novels, a story can be told by several characters, each presenting their point of view throughout the alternating chapters or scenes. This can also be accomplished in chapter books and middle grade books for older children; but changing the point of view is too confusing for young readers.

Three Types of Narrative

First-person narrative

Telling a story in *first-person narrative* means that the story is being told by a character—most often the main character—who will describe the thoughts and actions of all of the characters throughout the story. When choosing first-person narrative, it's imperative for you to be in close touch with the narrator's personality. Although other characters will be taking part in the dialogue within the story, only the narrator will *tell* the story. You are hearing the entire story from the narrator's point of view.

First-person narrative will use the pronouns *I, my, me, mine, our, myself, we, us.*

In this type of narrative, the main character must be interesting enough, and have the right personality to tell the story. Often stories are narrated by an animal, or even an inanimate object. For example, a dog can tell what it was like to be adopted; a fish can tell the sad story of coming in contact with the plastic ocean; a race car can even tell how difficult it is to be the smallest car in the race. First-person narration works best if the voice and words are believable.

If your main character has a distinct personality, perhaps overly silly, funny or quirky, a first-person narrative will offer the ability to make that character shine. Additionally, if your character has a lot to say, this will eliminate the potential overuse of dialogue and quotation marks.

It is usually not a good idea to have the main character/narrator be an adult whose role is to teach the children in the story a lesson. Young readers prefer to learn from the actions and voices of the young characters themselves.

> **Important note:** If you are writing a book for toddlers that features different characters throughout, you *can* have each character narrate their own page, saying, "I'm a bunny" or "I'm a kitten." This is perfectly acceptable.

Examples of first-person narrative:
- I think I'll go to Dylan's house to play today.
- I saw a huge snowman today.
- Billie is angry. I hope he finds his missing train set.
- I told Sally to put on her coat and go home.
- I'm such a cute puppy. Why won't anyone adopt me?
- I'm the sloppiest pig in the puddle.

Second-person narrative
When telling a story in *second-person narrative*, the person writing the story is the narrator and is speaking directly to the reader, often offering advice or giving instructions. This type of narrative is used less often than the others; however, it is popular in interactive books, which are typically board books and other toddler books. It is also used in instructional books.

Second-person narrative will use the pronouns *you, your, yours, yourself, yourselves.*

Examples of second person narrative:
- When you wash your hands, be sure to use soap.
- Your friends care about you, so don't be a bully.
- What do you think the puppy is doing?
- Now clap your hands and twirl around.

Third-person narrative
Telling a story in *third-person narrative* means the story is told by an outside voice that does not belong to any of the characters, but tells everything that is happening. This narrator has the ability to see, hear, and know what all of the characters are saying, thinking, and doing. This is the most common choice by authors of children's books; however, the challenge to the author is that the narrator has to know each character well enough to get their individual qualities and emotions across to the reader. That means that *you*, the writer, must know these characters well.

Third-person narrative will use the pronouns *he, his, himself, she, hers, herself, they, its, itself, theirs, them, themselves,* or the characters' names.

Examples of third-person narrative:
- Sally went to the pet shop.
- He said, "Nope, I'm not going."
- She did it all by herself.
- Timmy took his new truck to school.
- Billie didn't want to go outside.

Choosing one narrative

When you begin to write your story, a valuable exercise is to write the first few paragraphs in several different narratives. For most books, you will be choosing between first-person and third-person narrative. Then choose the point of view that feels most comfortable for you and your characters, and stick with it throughout the story.

"A passenger on a road journey is in the hands of a driver; a reader embarking on a book is in the hands of a narrator."
—Romesh Gunesekera

18

The Important Use of Dialogue

Dialogue is the conversation that allows the characters to use their voices to help tell the story. Dialogue makes a story more interesting and engaging. Without it, a story is merely a narration, and for young readers, listening to narration often becomes terribly boring. Many of us have known children who simply *tune us out* when we talk too much. We have watched their eyes glaze over as our words become nothing more than *blah, blah, blah*.

Be sure to achieve a balance.
It's important to achieve a comfortable balance between dialogue and narration in a story. Too much dialogue can become chatter; too much narration can slow the action and make a story monotonous.

You have too much dialogue if:
- you are using it for *small talk* that doesn't add to the story.
- you have more than four exchanges in any one conversation.
- your characters are making insignificant comments, such as *okay*.
- you have a character who is talking incessantly.

Why Dialogue is Important

Conversation is easy to listen to.

When someone is speaking (and saying something relevant), the reader has a reason to perk up and listen. The appropriate use of dialogue says, "Listen, I'm talking."

Dialogue gives us a window into the characters' personalities.

A few words of dialogue can offer a lot of information about a character's attitude and mood.

> **Example:**
> Instead of the narrator being the one to say that *Tommy is angry and doesn't want to ride his bike today,* let Tommy tell it his way: "I don't want to ride that ugly old bike anymore."

Be careful using dialogue when characters are thinking.

Even though dialogue can also be used to tell the reader what the character is thinking, too much thinking often means that the character needs another character to talk to. If every conversation ends with *he thinks* or *she thought,* you may need to give this character a friend.

Dialogue moves the story forward.

The use of dialogue is often more interesting than prolonged narration; it provides important information about the plot without lengthy descriptions. In children's daily routines, they are much more attuned to listening than reading.

In the following example, notice how much information is given about the characters and the plot, using just three lines of dialogue to move the story forward:

> *"Mom, I don't want you to turn the light off,"*
> *whispers Annie.*
>
> *"Why not, honey?"*
>
> *"I won't be able to see the monster if he comes*
> *again."*

If we were to write the same three lines of dialogue as narration, they would tell you:

> *Annie wants the light left on because she is*
> *afraid of the dark. She whispers so the monster*
> *can't hear her. Mom is sensitive to Annie's fears,*
> *but Annie is afraid that the monster might come*
> *again.*

You can see that the dialogue is much more effective than the narration in expressing the emotions of the characters. Instead of being told that Annie is afraid of the dark, let the reader learn from Annie's own voice as she whispers her fears to her mother.

Dialogue gives each character its own unique voice.
In children's books, it's important that the characters talk the way children actually talk. If you are a teacher, or have children of your own, you will be familiar with this concept. If not, you can learn how children communicate by volunteering to read to groups of children at a nearby school or library.

Engage the children in conversation, ask them questions—and pay attention to their different attitudes and ways of expressing themselves. In my own focus groups, I often do an exercise in which I read a line of dialogue and ask each child how *they* would say it differently.

When writing your characters' words, be sure the words are age-appropriate. Then make each character's words and tone unique. Just the way all children think and speak differently, your characters each need their own voice. What the characters say will tell the reader who they are. You can use the characters' words to make them sound sarcastic, angry, silly, sad or funny.

Read each of the following lines out loud. Notice the difference in tone, or voice, in each line:

- "I know just what to do. No one has to tell me anything!"
- "Maybe if I wish hard enough, a tiny fairy will visit me in my dreams tonight."
- "I miss my goldfish so much. Why did she have to go to fish heaven?"
- "Oh, really? What makes her think she's smarter than me?"
- "Isn't her outfit ridiculous?"

Dialogue defines the relationship between characters.
In addition to defining the characters' personalities, dialogue defines the way the characters interact with each other.

Notice the tone of the interaction between the characters below:

Brother and sister:

"Casey, pick up all that smelly junk!" his sister said, holding her nose.

"That's not junk, and it smells better than your silly perfume."

Mom and son:

"Mom, can I play outside on my new swing set today?"

"Sure, honey, but be sure to stay where I can see you."

Dialogue is a gift to adults.
Young children who are being read to by adults enjoy hearing the characters' different voices. When adults read in a variety of voices, the vocal drama can turn a simple storytime into an interactive and engaging experience for the adults, as well as the children.

What if the main character is also the narrator?

If the main character is the narrator, this means the story is being told in first-person narrative. (See Chapter 17: *Every Story Needs a Narrator*.) It also means that you will not use dialogue the same way that you would if the story was being told in third-person narrative. In this case, the narrator is the one who is talking to the reader; therefore, it is the narrator's job to orchestrate the dialogue and tell the reader who is talking and what they are saying.

Important: If Dylan is the narrator, you can never end a line of dialogue with *Dylan said.*

Examples of using dialogue when the narrator is talking:

- As I walked down the street I heard someone say, "Please play with me."
- I'll just go up to her and say, "You are being silly."
- Billy and Milly were arguing again. Billy said, "Give me my baseball."

The Use of Dialogue Tags

A dialogue tag is the *he said, she said* part of the sentence. It offers added description by telling us who is talking, and even offers insight into their mindset.

Examples:
- "It's time for me to go home," Ben **said.**
- "It's time for me to go home!" Ben **shouted.**
- "It's time for me to go home?" Ben **asked.**

Now a warning: It's best to keep it simple. If you use too many different descriptors, such as *he said, she cried, he exclaimed, she hollered,* it becomes nothing but noise and the story fades into the shadows.

Also, while people can shout and holler and whisper words, they do not laugh or snort words. It is correct to say: "I missed the step," Ben said, laughing. It is not correct to say: "I missed the step," Ben laughed.

A dialogue tag is not always needed.
Not every line of dialogue needs a *he said* or *she said*. In the following example, it becomes obvious who is talking, so a dialogue tag isn't needed in each line.

> "Mr. Turtle, would you like to swim with me?" asked the lobster.
>
> "No thanks, I'm not allowed to play with strangers."
>
> "But we already know each other, silly!"

Just be careful when omitting dialogue tags; only use this technique with 2 or 3 consecutive sentences. The reason is that too much back and forth can be confusing for young readers, and they will have trouble figuring out who is talking. And remember, the illustrations can also play a part in showing exactly who is speaking.

Adverbs can be added—sparingly.
Adverbs are descriptive words that tell us how, why, where, or when something happens. When used with dialogue, adverbs tell us *how* the character is speaking.

The use of an adverb after a dialogue tag can add more description:

• "It's time for me to go home," Jenny said **quietly.**

• "It's time for me to go home!" Jenny shouted **eagerly.**

• "It's time for me to go home!" Jenny hollered **angrily.**

Keep the adverbs in your toolbox, but remember to use them sparingly. Too many in one story will sound tedious and overused.

"The only dialogue that needs to be in your story is dialogue that (1) moves the plot forward, (2) develops characters, or (3) preferably both."
                                              —K. M. Weiland

19

Past Tense or Present Tense?

Children's books are almost always written in either *past tense* or *present tense.* Either tense will work well for telling a story, and either tense will work whether an outside narrator is telling the story or one of the characters is the narrator.

Note: There are actually three tenses: *past, present,* and *future*; and there are four different aspects of each tense: *simple, progressive, perfect,* and *perfect progressive,* but for our purposes, we will explore the two tenses most commonly used in children's books.

So how do you choose which tense is best for *your* book? If you are undecided, you might start by asking yourself an important question: Am I writing about something that happened in the past, or is my story unfolding right now?

Past Tense

As the name indicates, *past tense* means that the narrator is telling a story that happened in the past. Past tense works whether you have one of the characters telling the story or you are using an outside narrator. I like to think of past tense as a *once upon a time* story.

Stories written in past tense use verbs that normally end in *ed:* walked, hopped, listened, talked, chopped, hurried, hugged, jumped, etc. There are other past tense verbs that do not end with *ed*: *ran, found, saw, had, heard, fell,* etc. All of these words describe actions that happened in the past.

Examples of past tense:
- Billie *ran* quickly to the playground.
- Last winter we *had* a big snowstorm.
- Jamie *fell* off his bike.
- "I *went* fishing," said Dad, "and we *caught* lots of fish."
- We *saw* the cutest puppies in the pet shop.

Pros and Cons of Past Tense

Pros:
- This is the best way to tell a story that happened in the past.
- The reader learns the lesson that the characters have already learned, making the character's journey feel safe and secure.
- It allows the writer to reveal the back story.

Cons:
- Events happening in the distant past may seem too distant to young readers. To the youngest readers, the past barely goes beyond *yesterday.*
- Young children live in the present, and do not typically understand concepts such as: *when I was a child, when he grew to be a man, back before there were cars,* etc.

Present Tense

As the name indicates, *present tense* means the narrator is telling a story that is unfolding at the present time. As with past tense, present tense will work whether one of the characters or an outside narrator is telling the story.

Stories written in *present tense* do not have the *ed* ending that is used in past tense. Instead, present tense uses verbs that normally end in *s* when referring to an individual's actions: Billie walks, Jane hops, Tommy listens.

There is no *s* when referring to more than one person: Billie and his brother walk, Jane and June hop, Tommy and his dog listen.

There is no *s* when the narrator is carrying out the action: I walk to the store, I throw the ball in the air, I wonder which way to go.

Examples of *present tense*:
- Billie *runs* to the corner as fast as he can.
- As he *steers* his bike, he *hopes* he doesn't fall.
- I *dart* down the street and *hop* on the bus.
- I *steer* the boat carefully so I won't *fall* in the water.

Pros and Cons of Present Tense

Pros:
• Young children live in the present. Their understanding of past and future is typically limited to *yesterday* and *tomorrow*.
• Children like to feel as though they are living in the story.
• Children quickly identify with the characters and enjoy the excitement of sharing the characters' experiences.

Cons:
• It is a bit more difficult to write than *past tense*.
• It usually prevents you from having the story take place over a period of time.
• It may diminish the use of dialogue.

Warning: Avoid the Use of Past Perfect Tense

Past perfect tense is when you talk about something that happened before something else. It indicates that an action was completed at some point in the past.

Past perfect tense involves the use of the words *would, would have, would always, has, had, has been* and *had always.* My reason for mentioning this tense is to offer a suggestion: Avoid using it. While past perfect tense is widely used in adult books, young children are only able to grasp what is happening now and what has already happened. The concept of what *would* have happened is confusing, and the use of *has always* happened is unnecessary. Children's stories are *tighter* without this tense.

Examples of ways to avoid using past perfect tense:

- The happy puppy *has* chewed the blanket —>
  It looks like the puppy chewed the blanket.

- He *would always* go fishing with Dad. —>
  He loved to go fishing with Dad.

- I *had been* playing all afternoon. —>
  I played all afternoon.

- I *would have* liked to have gone to camp. —>
  I wanted to go to camp.

Mixing tenses

Does it work to mix tenses in one story? In adult novels, mixing past and present tense works well and is useful in adding understanding by providing back story about the characters or situation. It doesn't work well for children's books. Young children have trouble flipping back and forth from past to present; they have little understanding or concept of the past, and adding back story interrupts the story flow and causes confusion.

Here is an example of the beginning of a story written in past tense and then in present tense:

Past tense

Billie was a boy who loved boats. "One day I will build my own boat," he said to his dog Rocky. Rocky went everywhere with the boy and seemed to under-stand what the boy was saying.

Together, the pair gathered pieces of old wood that they found lying on the beach. Some of the wood was wet, so they spread it out to dry in the sun. Just then, they heard a loud clap of thunder. They ran home as fast as they could.

Billie yelled for his mother.

Present tense

"I love boats! One day I will build my own boat," Billie says to his dog Rocky. Rocky looks up at Billie as if he understands what Billie is saying.

The pair gather pieces of old wood that they see lying on the beach. Some of the wood feels wet, so Billie spreads it out to dry in the sun. Suddenly they hear a loud clap of thunder.

They run home as fast as they can.

"Mom!" Billie shouts.

Choosing one tense over another.

If you are ready to write your story and are unsure whether to choose past tense or present tense, try writing your first few paragraphs each way. Then decide which one helps you tell your story in the most clear and comfortable way.

"The past, present and future walked into a bar. It was tense."

—*Lex Martin*

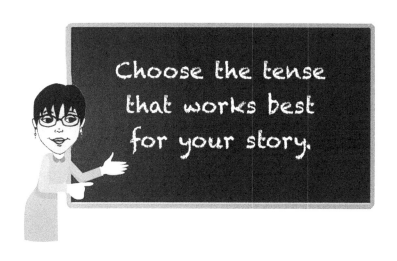

20
Writing Nonfiction Books

The definition of fiction is: a story in which the characters and storyline are created from the author's imagination; an invented story.

> **Examples:** Fairy tales and books about imaginary characters, such as *Cinderella, Harry Potter* and *Charlotte's Web*

The definition of nonfiction is: stories that are written about facts and real events, rather than imaginary ones.

> **Examples:** Books about science, history, travel, diversity, and famous people

Nonfiction books for children are always in demand, especially by educators. Contrary to what many people think, nonfiction books are not always biographies or memoirs, nor are they mini encyclopedias. Nonfiction stories can even be written in rhyme if the author chooses to do so. *Early concept books* for preschoolers, such as those dealing with colors and shapes, are actually nonfiction books.

What are Nonfiction STEM Books?

One of the most popular types of nonfiction books in today's market are STEM books.
The term STEM has become familiar to most students, teachers and parents. STEM is an acronym for four closely-connected areas of study: science, technology, engineering and mathematics. These fields are tied together in school curriculums due to the similarities they share, both in theory and in practice. STEM books can be written for children in every age group, from preschoolers to college graduates. STEM concepts can be incorporated into every type of children's book, from board books through middle grade books.

Even preschoolers can be introduced to stories that explore Scientific inquiry, Technological challenges, Engineering ideas, and Mathematical experiences. When building a tower, learning to count their blocks, measuring their height, understanding weather patterns, or learning why the leaves are turning yellow, STEM concepts are being introduced.

If this is your niche and you are looking for a STEM topic for your book, the list is endless. For example, just a few popular topics geared to elementary schools are: weather, beekeeping, space travel, chemistry experiments, how things work, how things grow, the environment, recycling, animals, nature...etc. The list is endless.

Choose a nonfiction topic that children will enjoy.

Children are curious creatures; they love books about things they've never heard of, so be sure to explore the interests of the children in your target audience. One way to do this is to talk to a few elementary teachers. Another way is to visit a library and/or bookstore for a firsthand look at the most popular nonfiction books. If there's a particular topic that interests you, make sure it will also interest your target audience. For example, *you* might love everything about statistics, and it is definitely math-oriented, but will this be of interest to children?

Numerous topics can be adapted to multiple age groups.

How deeply you delve into a topic for a nonfiction book depends on your target audience. For example, if you decide to write a story about bees, you can adapt this subject to fit your audience.

Your choices may be to:
- write a *board book* with simple illustrations of a bee, a hive and flowers.
- write a *picture book* with a character who is learning from his beekeeping neighbor how bees make honey.
- write a *middle grade book* stressing the facts about bees and how their existence is being threatened.
- write a factual account for middle school students about bees and other insects that are being sent into space.

Research is important.
Nonfiction books require three types of research:

(1) Find out how many books have already been published on your topic. Some topics have been covered repeatedly in many forms and from many different angles, so doing your research will help you find a different way to approach a topic to make it unique.

(2) Once you have chosen your topic, you owe it to your readers to gain as much knowledge as you possibly can. It may be a subject that you know well, and that's always a plus, but further research is always helpful. There is a lot of information available online, but be sure to choose your sources carefully and only rely on credible websites for your information.

(3) Make absolutely sure that your story is written with the appropriate vocabulary and language that your target audience will understand. Be certain that the concept is not too advanced, or too simplistic, for your particular age group. A trip to the library and a focus group of children will be of great help.

Adding *back matter* to a nonfiction book.
It is often helpful to add educational materials, such as a glossary or teacher's guide, to the back of a nonfiction book. A list of other available resources on your topic is also useful. The back matter is often in the form of related questions and recommended activities for teachers and/or parents to engage in with the children.

What is Narrative Nonfiction?

Narrative nonfiction, also called *creative nonfiction,* weaves fictional elements into a factual story. Rather than simply stating facts about a topic, a bit of fiction often helps in highlighting the message. With creative nonfiction, the goal is not only to inform, but to also entertain. Similar to other fiction books, these stories still need to contain the required elements of character development, plot, narrative, tense and dialogue (covered in previous chapters).

Examples of creative narrative nonfiction.
The theoretical examples below illustrate ways that you can weave fiction and nonfiction together:

• **The Biggest Bug.** Readers can learn about a bug's features and habitat as they follow along with the character who is trailing *the biggest bug ever.*

• **A visit to the International Space Station.** A story can follow a fictional character through the preparation and eventual journey into outer space.

• **How to build a nest.** Readers can learn how birds build nests, and watch the actual building process take place as the story is narrated by talking birds.

• **How much money do I need?** Readers can learn how to count their allowance while saving for a special toy.

• **Can I eat half a pie?** Readers can gain an understanding of fractions when seeing how the characters cut and share their pies (or pizzas).

• **What shape is that?** Children in the story can guess the shapes that a character is drawing on the sidewalk.

• **Let's build a bridge.** This can be a step-by-step building project that the main character witnesses or participates in.

If you are under the impression that nonfiction books are boring, think again!

"The challenge of nonfiction is to marry art and truth."
—Phyllis Rose

Nonfiction books are more popular than ever.

21
Writing a Series

Turning a book into a series is a path to consider, especially if your first book has been successful and you feel that you have a lot of story left to tell. Plus, the release of a new book will often revive the life of an existing book and greatly expand your fan base. One important thing to remember: When creating a successful series, consistency is the key.

How to Maintain Consistency in a Series

Characters

The main character
It's important for the main character to remain consistent throughout the series. If you have more than one main character, they can either share the spotlight or take turns playing a dominant role. For example, you may have a story about Jake and his sister Lucy, with Jake being the protagonist in some of the books, then Lucy taking center stage in others. In this case, both characters should appear in each book in the series.

If the main character is Henry the Superhero, you would keep him in place throughout the series; however, you can add a brand new character in each book who can come onto the scene to interact with Henry. You would continue with the same main character and the same superhero theme.

If there are additional characters in the story, they may or may not always be necessary to the storyline; however, they do add continuity, so you may want to keep one or two of them around.

Characters' appearance and age
When moving the characters into a new story, it's important to keep their physical features the same. If the character has long blonde hair and blue eyes in the first book, don't have her showing up in the next book with brown hair and brown eyes. Also, the unique nature of the character needs to remain strong and consistent throughout the series.

Should the characters grow older in future books? If your books are geared to the younger readers, the answer is *no*. When children read the series out of order, as they often do, any big difference in the age or appearance of the character will be confusing.

With chapter books or middle grade books, which will reach older readers, more time can pass as the series progresses, and children can age. An example of this is the Harry Potter series, in which the characters grow older with each book.

Theme

What is the theme (underlying message) of your series? Consistency can be maintained by having the theme remain the same, even though each adventure can be different. For example, if a character is exploring a possible future occupation in one book, he might discover a different occupation in each additional book. If the character learns a new skill in the first book, he can learn another new skill in each additional book. The theme might also be something like finding courage, meeting a new animal, or exploring a new country, but the format needs to be consistent.

While this type of predictable formula often becomes boring in adult novels, children are excited about seeing what trouble their adored character will get into, or what he will discover in the next book.

Setting

There are two popular choices to select from when planning the setting for future stories:
(1) Tell a different story from the same setting.
(2) Move the same cast of characters to a new location.

The latter method is more popular, with most authors finding it easier to weave a new tale when relocating the characters to a different setting. For example, Kendra can go hiking in one story and to the zoo in another. Either way, it's important that some of the elements remain familiar within each new story—such as Kendra's same best friend or the fact that Kendra goes everywhere on her blue bike or likes to wear red shirts.

Format

All of the books in a series should be the same size and format, such as paperback or hardcover, square or rectangular. Aside from looking more uniform, they will stack together nicely on a shelf and will also give your series a distinct look.

Length

The books in a series should all be close to the same length. An extra page or two is fine, but pairing a book of three hundred words and 32 pages with one of nine hundred words and 44 pages should be avoided.

Illustrations

If possible, work with the same illustrator for each book. If this isn't possible, find an illustrator who can work in the same style and medium as in the original book. Young readers need to be able to easily recognize the characters.

Cover

Plan for some degree of continuity with the book covers. You may wish to have the same color scheme on each book. In this case, if the main character is featured on each cover, just be sure that the character is doing something different on each new book.

Another choice is to have each cover created in a different color. Even children who have not yet learned to read are often able to identify each book in the series by its color.

Working with the same cover designer, illustrator, and graphic designer will make cover continuity easier to accomplish. Let your team know if you are thinking of doing a series so they can help you plan ahead for your future books.

Other Things to Consider

There's no need to repeat.
It's not necessary to recount every detail of what happened in the previous book. You can allude to something that happened in the last book, as long as it is woven into the story so it doesn't feel out of place. Children are smart; they will catch up. Realistically, there is the possibility that your second book will be the first book of your series that a child reads, so it's important for each book to have the strength to stand alone.

Plan ahead.
If you think a series is right for your characters, it would be best to plan a structural outline for all of the books while you are working on the first story. Formulating your future strategy will help you as you create each new adventure. It will make it easier to plan the characters' actions and reactions, and will keep you on track as you create each new book.

Develop a release schedule.
It's generally best to release each book within a year of the previous book, enabling you to keep up momentum before your previous book is forgotten. It's often wise to try to release books in conjunction with gift-giving holidays if possible, especially if your theme ties into a specific celebration.

How many books comprise a series?

There is no magic number. You can write 2 books or 52 books—as long as each idea is fresh, your timing is right, and your fans are excited.

First, find out what your hero wants, then just follow him!"

—Ray Bradbury

22
Show, Don't Tell

Two important techniques that writers can utilize to communicate the essence of a story are *showing* and *telling*. With *showing*, the readers feel as if they are a part the story; with *telling*, the readers feel more like bystanders. It's important to understand the difference and learn how to use each of these techniques to your advantage.

Showing

Showing is a way to use descriptive words to make a story more lively and enjoyable. It adds highlights to a story by using words that appeal to the senses, thereby creating mental pictures that enhance the reading experience. It uses a character's action or dialogue to *show* the reader what a character is feeling (and doing).

In children's picture books, *showing* also refers to the use of illustrations to fulfill their role in reporting an important part of the story. This is one reason why, when choosing an illustrator, you should look for one who is able to communicate the characters' facial expressions and emotions as well as their actions.

Telling

In relation to a story, the simple definition of *telling* is: using flat descriptions to inform the reader what is happening or how a character is feeling. *Telling* by itself, without *showing*, can become a boring narrative. For children, the fun of using their imagination is spoiled by *telling* them everything they need to know.

Examples of Telling vs. Showing

Telling: *Amy was sad when she couldn't find her dog. She searched everywhere.*
Showing: *As she searched for Fluffy, Amy could hardly see through the tears running down her face.*

There is no need to *tell* the reader that Amy is sad. Let them come to that conclusion when they read that the tears are running down her face; let them feel the emotion as they read the words. The illustration should also *show* the sadness.

Telling: *Mom is busy. I think she is baking again.*
Showing: *The smell of butter and brown sugar filled the air. Amy knew it was Mom's cinnamon rolls—the ones with gooey vanilla icing.*

Simply saying that Mom is baking is a boring summary of what mom is doing. But smelling the aroma and tasting the gooey icing awakens the senses and creates imagery that is crystal clear.

Telling: *The house was spooky. They were afraid to enter.*
Showing: *The house was dark, except for an eerie sliver of moonlight shining through the ragged curtains. The air smelled like Grandma's attic, and the dust made him cough.*

In this example, adding the description *shows* the reader how the house looks, how it feels, and how it smells.

Telling: *I think someone is coming up behind me.*
Showing: *I hear the sound of crunching gravel as the footsteps get louder—and closer.*

In this example, appealing to the sense of hearing enables a reader to use their imagination to *hear* the crunching sounds.

Remember: Rather than simply describing the scenes and actions in your story, your goal should be to create a series of mental images that will draw your readers in and allow them to be a part of the experience. A combination of *showing* and *telling* is the key to a good story.

"Don't tell me the moon is shining: show me the glint of light on broken glass."
—Anton Chekhov

PART 5

How to Write a
Rhyming Story

23

To Rhyme or
Not to Rhyme

Children love the musicality of rhyme and the poetic use of the sound of words; however, that does not mean that every book should be written in rhyme. Not every writer is comfortable with rhyme—and that's fine. Not everyone can dance; some people stumble a lot when they can't feel the rhythm.

Most children's books are written in prose, so don't think of it as a second choice. Prose is beautiful in its own right; it can be as melodious, dramatic, and poetic as rhyme. Here are some important aspects to consider when making the decision whether or not to write your story in rhyme:

Does your story have an in-depth plot?
If this is the case, or if you are using multi-syllabic words, then rhyming may not work for you. The deeper your plot or message, and the more details you need in order to tell your story, the harder it will be to find the right rhyming words.

Not only are long words difficult to rhyme, but too many syllables can wreak havoc on your rhyming meter. Imagine trying to fit the following words into a rhyme: imagination, ridiculous, baseball stadium, dangerous, marathon, roller skates, refrigerator.

Disclaimer: This does not mean that no one should ever write a detailed story in verse. A number of successful rhyming books offer a lot of detail, yet still work beautifully.

Are you planning to have your book translated?
If you are publishing your own book and thinking ahead, and if there's a chance that you might want to have your book translated into other languages, creating a rhyming book will be difficult, if not impossible, to accomplish. It can be done, but in most cases the meaning of many of the words will change.

Will you be able to express your ideas clearly?
Rhyme should never be the force that drives the story. Often writers have a clear vision of what they wish to say, and want to write a rhyming story, but then find themselves unable to express their ideas as clearly as they had hoped. If the words they are using to tell their story are difficult to rhyme, writers are often compelled to change the words; thus, the initial meaning of the story may be lost.

What types of stories work best in rhyme?
More simplistic stories usually work well in rhyme. Stories with short words, simple plots and simple subjects are much easier to fit into a rhyming meter. Bedtime stories and lullabies also work well when written in soothing rhyme.

Quirky stories are often good candidates for rhyming books, and even allow authors to make up their own words. Dr. Seuss books are a perfect example—with original names like Yertle the Turtle and Circus McGurkus.

Are rhyming books just for toddlers?
Absolutely not. While it's true that rhyming books do help young children learn to read, even upper elementary children enjoy a good rhyming story—the quirkier, the better!

Do traditional publishers really dislike rhyming books?
Perhaps you've heard this rumor, but is it true? Yes and no. Publishers do not like *bad* rhyme, which includes issues such as lack of a consistent meter, the use of forced rhyme, and the lack of a cohesive, substantive story.

Publishers are also concerned about the inability to sell the foreign rights to books that may not translate well into other languages. That being said, if you plan to submit a rhyming book to a literary agent or publisher, be sure it is well written and professionally edited.

Ask yourself this question:
Am I totally committed to rhyme? Whether your answer is *yes* or *no*, here's a valuable first step: Write your story in prose (regular storytelling), expressing the feelings you would like to convey, developing the plot, and using the language you would like to use.

Then choose one of two paths:

(1) If the story works well, keep it in prose.

(2) Use the prose version as the base for a rhyming book. Just be sure you will be able to find rhyming words that will get your feelings and message across. In other words, don't sacrifice your story for the rhyme.

If you are seriously interested in writing in rhyme, do yourself a favor and read *a lot* of rhyming books before you begin.

The rhyme should not be the force that drives the story.

24
Learning to Rhyme Begins with *I Love You*

If you've ever danced to music, you know there is a beat to follow. You can follow the beat and be in sync, or skip a beat here and there and end up stepping on someone's toes. Similarly, before you can write in rhyme, you need to *feel the beat.* I will share with you one of my prompts for teaching prospective rhymers to do just that.

Here is a simple sentence: **I love you.** This little collection of three words can be read and interpreted in three different ways; it all depends on the word you choose to *stress,* or *emphasize.*

1. *I* love you. If you emphasize the *I* as you say it, it means that *I* am the one who loves you.

2. I *LOVE* you. If you emphasize the word *LOVE*, it means that within the range of feelings that exist in the world, this is how I feel about you.

3. I love *YOU*. If you emphasize the word *YOU*, it means that *you alone* are the one I love.

Once you can read *I Love You* three different ways, you will understand the meaning and use of stressed words and syllables in rhymes. This understanding will help you navigate the following chapters.

"How do I love thee? Let me count the ways...

—Elizabeth Barrett Browning

25

Understanding Rhyme Scheme

The term *rhyme scheme* refers to the *pattern* of rhyming words that comes at the *end* of each rhyming line. The pattern can be identified by using letters to indicate which lines rhyme. Think of it as the blueprint for creating your rhyme.

Finding the rhyme scheme is easy: Simply look at the *end rhyme*—the last word in each line. Keep in mind that lines do not have to be consecutive in order to rhyme.

Note: Rhyme scheme deals *only* with the end rhyme and has nothing to do with stressed or unstressed syllables.

In children's books, it's important to keep the rhyme scheme consistent throughout the story. Once a child catches on to the pattern, it may be confusing if the pattern changes; however, rhyme schemes *can* be mixed if done skillfully and in appropriate places. Dr. Seuss books provide excellent examples of successfully varied rhyme schemes.

The Three Most Commonly Used Rhyme Schemes in Children's Books

AABB, ABAB, ABCB

Remember that the rhyme scheme is simply looking at the *last words* in each line of rhyme.

AABB
In this pattern, the first 2 lines end with words that rhyme, creating a rhyme scheme of **AA.**

The next 2 lines end with words that make a different rhyme, creating a rhyme scheme of **BB.**

Together they create a rhyme scheme of **AABB.**
This is often called *coupled rhyme* because each pair of lines (**AA** or **BB**) is called a *couplet.*

Examples of AABB rhyme scheme:

Twinkle Twinkle little **star,**   A
How I wonder what you **are.**   A
Up above the world so **high.**   B
Like a diamond in the **sky.**   B

If I were you and you were **me,** A
Oh, how funny that would **be.**   A
But if I am me and you are **you,** B
Will we still know who is **who?** B

ABAB

In this pattern, the last word in the *first* and *third* lines rhyme. The last word in the *second* and *fourth* lines make a different rhyme.

Together they create a rhyme scheme of **ABAB**.

Examples of ABAB rhyme scheme:

The people along the **sand**   A
All turn and look one **way.**   B
They turn their back on the **land.** A
They look at the sea all **day.**   B
—Robert Frost

Are you going to Scarborough **Fair?**   A
Parsley, sage, rosemary, and **thyme.**   B
Remember me to one who lives **there.** A
For once she was a true love of **mine.**   B
—English Folk Song

ABCB

This pattern consists of a 4-line verse with the *second* and *fourth* lines rhyming. The *first* and *third* lines do *not* rhyme with any other lines.

Examples of ABCB rhyme scheme:

I'm a little teapot   A
Short and **stout**   B
Here is my handle **C**
Here is my **spout**   B
—George Harold Sanders

My sister is special, I know for a fact,	A
Even with her ridiculous **clothes**.	B
So of course, she just giggles whenever I ask,	C
How can you go out wearing **those?**	B

Additional Rhyme Schemes

In addition to the most popular rhyme schemes listed above, there are a number of others. Two of the more interesting ones that you might encounter are:

AABBA

This lively rhyme scheme is used in writing *limericks*, 5-line silly rhymes that tell a story. Limericks are fun to insert within a story, but are rarely used throughout an entire book.

Example of AABBA rhyme scheme:

There was once a young boy who was small.	A
And he dreamed that someday he'd be tall;	A
so he stood on a chair	B
and forgot to take care.	B
and now no one can see him at all.	A

There was an Old Man with a beard,	A
Who said, 'It is just as I feared!	A
Two Owls and a Hen,	B
Four Larks and a Wren,	B
Have all built their nests in my beard!'	A

—Edward Lear

AAAA

Known as *monorhyme,* this is a rhyme scheme in which every line rhymes. It is difficult, and usually monotonous, to write an entire story with the same end rhyme. One of the biggest hazards is running out of true rhyming words and then forcing or repeating the rhyme. It *can* work well, and add a cute effect, when written as a small section of rhyme within a larger story that is written in either rhyme or prose.

Examples of AAAA rhyme scheme:
Star light, star bright,   **A**
First star I see tonight,   **A**
I wish I may, I wish I might,   **A**
Have this wish I wish tonight.   **A**
                    —Jane Taylor

The woods are lovely, dark and deep, **A**
But I have promises to keep,   **A**
And miles to go before I sleep, **A**
And miles to go before I sleep. **A**
                    —Robert Frost

Remember: Once you have chosen a rhyme scheme for a children's story, it's important to stick with it. Changes in the rhyming pattern will throw the reader off and disrupt the flow of the story.

"Rhyme patterns are nothing without meanings to the words."
—J. Cole

26

Understanding Meter: How to Get the Beat

To some people, *meter* is a scary word. "I just don't get it," they say. So let's start from the beginning, break it down, and make it easy to understand.

What is meter?
Meter is the basic rhythmic beat of a line of rhyme; it is the pattern of stressed and unstressed syllables. Think about dancing to music; when you take a step with each strong beat, you are *feeling* the beat that is stressed.

Why does it matter? In children's books, it's important to keep the meter consistent throughout the story. Once a child catches on to the beat, changes in rhythm will be confusing.

The meter of a rhyme is determined by counting the stressed and unstressed syllables in each line. Each grouping of stressed and unstressed syllables is call a *metric foot*. Without meter, you simply have a group of sentences that end in rhyming words; but there is more to rhyming than that.

Understanding stressed and unstressed syllables
In English, every word is made up of stressed and
unstressed syllables. If a word has more than one
syllable, one of the syllables will be stressed; the
others will be unstressed.

Example #1: Say the word *wonderful* out loud.
Did you emphasize (put stress on) the first, second or
third syllable?
>**won** der ful
>won **der** ful
>won der **ful**

In the English language, we say **won** der ful. The
stress, or beat, is always on the first syllable in this
word.

Example #2: Say the word *thunder* out loud.
Did you emphasize the first or second syllable?
>**thun** der
>thun **der**

In the English language, we say **thun** der. The stress,
or beat, is always on the first syllable in this word.

There are a number of metric patterns, however we
will delve into the two that are most commonly used in
children's books. We will explore them in the next two
sections. Don't worry if you are seeing some of the terms
for the first time; the important thing to learn from the
following two chapters is to identify and *feel* the meter
rather than remember the name of each type.

You will definitely find it helpful to read the examples
out loud, and even clap your hands as you say each
stressed word or syllable.

Counting syllables

Many writers who are new to rhyme think that if every line of rhyme has the same number of syllables, that's all that counts. Wrong! What you must look at is the pattern of *stressed syllables* in each line. If that pattern is consistent, it is often fine to overlook an extra (or missing) unstressed syllable.

If you follow a pattern, you will end up with a syllable count that is similar in each line. Conversely, if you begin the process by simply creating lines with the same syllable count while paying no attention to the placement of the accented and unaccented syllables, your rhyme will lack consistency and will not flow. (See the next two chapters.)

26A
Anapestic Meter

Meter is the pattern of stressed and unstressed syllables in a line of rhyme. In children's books, it is important to keep the meter consistent throughout the story. Once a child catches on to the beat, changes in rhythm will be confusing.

One of the most commonly used meters is *anapestic meter*, which refers to a *metric foot (called an anapest)* consisting of two unstressed syllables followed by a stressed syllable. Anapestic meter has a lively feel that lends itself well to rhymes for children.

The words (or parts of words) that appear in **bold** print in the descriptions below represent the stressed beats. It may help to clap your hands as you read aloud the words or syllables that are stressed.

The following three-syllable words are *anapests,* with the stress on the third syllable.
The beat is: da-da-***DUM:***

interr**upt**, under***stand***, under***neath***

The following lines each contain two *anapestic feet.* This is called *anapestic dimeter.*

The beat is: da-da-***DUM*** da-da-***DUM:***

> So I ***ran*** to the ***top.***
> Then I ***bounced*** down the ***hall.***
>
> I am ***round*** and I ***glow.***
> I'm a ***big*** yellow ***ball.***
> .....
>
> "You have ***brains*** in your ***head,***"
> is what ***Doc***tor Seuss ***said.***

The following lines contain three *anapestic feet.* This is called *anapestic trimeter.*

The beat is: da-da-***DUM*** da-da-***DUM*** da-da-***DUM:***

> As she ***sits*** in the ***mud*** and she ***cries,***
> the rain ***wash***es the ***tears*** from her ***eyes.***
> .....
>
> There were ***two*** little ***cubs*** in the ***zoo.***
> They were ***named*** Little ***Jack*** and Big ***Boo.***

Important: Notice that in the verses on this page, the anapest is sometimes split within one word in order to form the three syllables (da-da-***DUM)*** that are needed to create the anapest. Notice how the word ***washes*** is split. Each syllable of this word is part of a different anapestic foot; however, when reading the entire line, you will see how the words flow together.

The following lines contain four *anapestic feet*. This is called *anapestic tetrameter*.

The beat is:
da-da-**DUM** da-da-**DUM** da-da-**DUM** da-da-**DUM:**

Twas the **night** before **Christ**mas and **all** through
the **house,**
Not a **crea**ture was **stir**ring, not **e**ven a **mouse.**
.....

As we **start**ed to **dress** for our **sleep**over **snooze**,
we put **on** our pa**jam**as and **took** off our **shoes.**

How to Make Anapestic Meter Work for YOU!

If this is your meter of choice, let's take a look at how to make it work. We begin with a rhyme that does not have any definite meter. (In fact, it's impossible to know which words to stress when reading it):

> *He scooted very quickly into my room,*
> *then he began tossing my toys all over the floor.*
> *He didn't care about cleaning anything up,*
> *because he just threw more.*

Let's change a few words, rearrange others, and give each line the anapestic rhythm of: da-da-**DUM** da-da-**DUM** da-da-**DUM** (anapestic trimeter). At the same time, we need to retain the meaning of the original verse:

> Then he **scoot**ed so **fast** to my **room**,
> tossing **toys** all a**round** the clean **floor**.
> I could **tell** he would **not** clean them **up**.
> He just **kept** throwing **more**... and then **more**.

You can even vary the rhyme by keeping the same meter, while alternating the number of anapestic feet in each line. The number at the end of each line indicates the number of stressed syllables in that particular line.

Then he **scoot**ed as **fast** as he **could** to my **room**, (**4**)
tossing **toys** all ar**ound** the clean **floor**. (**3**)
I could **tell** he would **not** care at **all** to clean **up**. (**4**)
He just **kept** throwing **more**... and then **more**. (**3**)

The important takeaway: Once you feel the beat, in this case da-da-**DUM,** you need to stick to it throughout your story. If you find it necessary to change some of the words in order to keep the beat, be absolutely sure that the words still have the intended meaning.

I enjoy writing rhymes and sitting alone in a room listening to beats. It's pretty amazing.
—Joaquin Phoenix

26B
Iambic Meter

Another commonly used meter is *iambic meter*, which refers to a *metric foot* consisting of two syllables, with the stress on the second syllable. You can think of iambic meter as having the rhythm of a heartbeat.

Remember: In children's books, it's important to keep the meter consistent throughout the story. Once a child catches on to the beat, changes in rhythm will be confusing.

The words (or parts of words) that appear in **bold** print in the descriptions below represent the stressed beats. It may help to clap your hands as you read aloud the words or syllables that are stressed.

The following two-syllable words are *iambs,* with the stress on the second syllable.

The beat is: da-***DUM:***
    be***long,*** de***cide,*** de***vice***

The following lines contain 2 *iambic feet*. This is called *iambic dimeter*.

The beat is: da-***DUM*** da-***DUM:***

When ***up*** a***loft***
I ***fly*** and fly
I ***see*** in ***pools***
The ***shin***ing ***sky***

I ***stand*** and ***look***
And ***stop*** and ***drink***
And ***bathe*** my ***wings***
And ***chink***, and ***pink***.
    —**Thomas Hardy**
    .....

The ***fall***ing ***snow***.
Just ***makes*** me ***glow***.
    .....

I'd ***love*** to ***run***
Up ***to*** the ***sun***.

Important: Notice that the iamb is sometimes split within one word in order to form the two syllables (da-***DUM)*** that are needed to form the iamb. Notice how the word ***shining*** is split. Each syllable of the word is part of a different iambic foot; however, when reading the entire line, you will see how the words flow together.

The following lines contain three *iambic feet*. This is called *iambic trimeter*. It is short and bouncy and works well with simple stories.

The beat is: da-**DUM** da-**DUM** da-**DUM:**

> I *heard* the *teach*er *say.*
> Don't *throw* your *lunch* a*way.*
> But *I* was *feel*ing *smart.*
> I *on*ly *saved* my *tart.*
>
> .....
>
> We *romped* un*til* the *pans*
> Slid *from* the *kitch*en s*helf;*
> My *moth*er's *count*en*ance*
> Could *not* un*frown* it*self.*
> —Theodore Roethke

The following lines contain four *iambic feet*. This is called *iambic tetrameter*.

The beat is: da-**DUM** da-**DUM** da-**DUM** da-**DUM:**

> I *wan*dered, *lone*ly *as* a *cloud*
> That *floats* on *high* o'er *dales* and *hills*
> When, *all* at *once*, I *saw* a *crowd*
> A *host* of *gold*en *daff*o*dils.*
> —William Wordsworth
>
> .....
>
> So *long* a*go* and *far* a*way,*
> Two *fair*ies *came* to *town* one *day.*
> The *kids* all *loved* them *from* the *start*
> Be*cause* each *had* a *big*, kind *heart.*

The following lines contain five *iambic feet*. This is called *iambic pentameter*. When most writers think of iambic pentameter, they immediately associate this meter with William Shakespeare. He often used this meter in his writing, and was adept at combining iambic pentameter with other meters.

The beat is:
da-*DUM* da-*DUM* da-*DUM* da-*DUM* da-*DUM:*

> I *wish* I *were* a *mon*ster *kind* of **guy**,
> A *shag*gy, *bag*gy *mon*ster *with* one *eye*.
> To *look* me *in* the *eye* might *cause* a *fright*,
> But *don't* be *scared*; you *see*, I'd *nev*er *bite*.
> .....

But *soft,* what *light* through *yon*der *win*dow *breaks?*
>   —William Shakespear*e*

>   .....

If *mu*sic *be* the *food* of *love*, play *on*;
>   —William Shakespeare

Iambic meter has a regularity to it that enables both writers and young readers to *feel the beat* and get in step with the words. It works with both long and short sentences, making it easy to use with one-, two-, and even three-syllable words.

How to Make Iambic Meter Work For YOU!

If this is your meter of choice, let's see how to make it work for you. Let's begin with a rhyme that does not have any definite rhythm; in fact, it's impossible to know which words to stress when reading it:

She bolted very quickly in through the door,
then she began slopping mud all over my house.
The mud was on her face and her hair,
and she even managed to get it on my blouse.

Let's change a few words and rearrange others to give each line a da-***DUM*** rhythm. At the same time, we need to keep the meaning of the original verse. The number at the end of each line indicates the number of stressed syllables in that particular line.

She **bolt**ed **quick**ly **through** the **door**, (4)
slopped **mud** a**round** my **house**. (3)
It's **on** her **face** and **in** her **hair**, (4)
and **now** it's **on** my **blouse**! (3)

We have also varied the rhyme by alternating the number of iambic feet in each line. This illustrates the flexibility you have once you decide on a meter. This pattern alternates lines containing 4 iambs with lines of 3 iambs.

Here's another example of varying the number of iambic feet in a rhyme:

If **all** the **world** were **ap**ple **pie**, **(4)**
And **all** the **sea** were **ink**, **(3)**
And **all** the **trees** were **bread** and **cheese**, **(4)**
What **should** we **do** for **drink**? **(3)**
                                    —Nursery rhyme

The important takeaway: Once you feel the beat, in this case da-***DUM,*** you need to stick to it throughout your story. If you find it necessary to change words in order to keep the beat, make sure the words still have the intended meaning.

"I've spent so much time with iambic pentameter that I can now recognize it when I hear it in conversation or a movie - it's like a weird, useless superpower."
                                    —Ian Doescher

Iambic meter has the rhythm of a heartbeat: da-DUM

27
How to Punctuate a Rhyming Story

In children's stories, the purpose of each sentence is to offer information. Rhyming stories are no different. Therefore, to provide clarity and understanding for young readers, punctuation is important. Most of the time it's best to go with the normal punctuation that you would use in writing prose.

There is one important caveat to keep in mind regarding the use of punctuation in a rhyme: Be certain that the rhyming meter is not interrupted by the pause that the punctuation adds to a line.

Use normal punctuation.
If a comma is needed, use a comma. The same goes for an apostrophe, colon, or semi-colon. They are used to show a separation of ideas or thoughts within the line. Use these punctuation marks judiciously because they create a slight pause in the forward movement of the rhyme. An em dash (—) can be used for emphasis, however it's important to understand that its effect is also the creation of a pause in a line of text.

Don't be afraid to use a period in the middle of a line
if the sentence ends there. An exclamation mark or
question mark can be used, but keep in mind that they
create a stronger pause than a period.

Example:
I'll tell you a story. I think it is true!
It was told by a fairy. I'll tell it to you.

An ellipsis is sometimes used at the end of a line as an
indication that there is more to come.

Example:
Here they come around the bend...
the kitty and her new best friend.

Quotation marks are used when there is dialogue in
a verse, just the way you would use them in writing
prose.

Examples:
Billy said, "I just won't go."
Then he added, "NO, NO, NO!"

.....

"Let's hold hands," she says lightly, and then very soon
she says, "Let's make a wish by the light of the moon."

.....

Not every line needs punctuation at the end.
End a line with a period (or question mark or
exclamation mark) only if it is the logical end of the
sentence. Keep in mind that the end of a rhyming line
is not always the end of a thought; therefore it may not
require punctuation.

It is often obvious to the reader that the sentence is not complete when there is no punctuation at the end of the line. When a thought runs from one line to another, this is called *enjambment*. Enjambment allows lines to move smoothly and fit the rhyming scheme. It adds variety and also allows young readers to move more quickly to the next line to follow the thought.

> **Examples of enjambment:**
> I think that I shall never see
> a poem as lovely as a tree.
> — Joyce Kilmer
> .....

> Whether 'tis nobler in the mind to suffer
> the slings and arrows of outrageous fortune ...
> —William Shakespeare
> .....

> You do not have to be
> as small as a mouse
> to fit in my pocket and
> hide in my house.

Should every line of rhyme begin with a capital letter?

There are two schools of thought when it comes to using capitalization in a rhyming story. One is an older, more traditional way, while the other is a newer, more relaxed way. Many people still adhere to the older norm of automatically capitalizing the first word of each line of verse, however there is no written rule for this. It is becoming less common, and often depends on the rhyme itself.

If a capital letter interrupts a sentence, it may become a distraction to young readers, who are taught that capital letters begin a new thought.

There are many writers today who still use initial capital letters, and others who do not. The important element to consider when making the decision is the clarity of the story. Whichever path you choose, be sure to remain consistent throughout the story.

Here is an example of the same rhyme written with and without initial capital letters:

With:
With all of the noise,
The kids woke from their sleep.
Their tummies were rumbling
From way, way down deep.

Without:
With all of the noise,
the kids woke from their sleep.
Their tummies were rumbling
from way, way down deep.

Grammar and punctuation rules are loosening since "the old days," allowing writers and book formatters to make their own stylistic choices. You will be fine if you remain consistent, do the best you can, then hire a professional editor to help you fine-tune your manuscript.

"I'm tired of wasting letters when punctuation will do, period."
—Steve Martin

Not every
rhyming line
needs punctuation
at the end.

28

Rhyming Language: Be Careful of the Pitfalls

Understanding rhyme scheme and meter is of great importance, but that's not all there is to writing a successful rhyming story. There's also the *language* to consider. Knowing the difference between *perfect rhyme* and *near rhyme,* and knowing how to write rhyming lines for your target audience, will vastly improve your overall ability to write a story that children will love.

Tailor the language to your target audience.
When we think of the language of the famous poets, we often think of beautiful, flowing lines of descriptive adjectives and flowery words, but let's bring that down to earth. People speak differently today.

Example:
Let's look at Shakespeare's famous line:

"Good Night, Good night! Parting is such sweet sorrow, that I shall say good night till it be morrow."

If written today, those words might be boiled down to:
"Good night, my friend. I'll miss you tonight. Let's meet again when the sun is bright."

When you write a rhyming story for children, it is imperative that your audience understand what you are saying. Just as in a story written in prose, the words in a rhyming story must make sense to your target audience. (And don't forget the story's requisite beginning, middle and end.)

Strive for perfect rhyme.
The definition of *perfect rhyme* is: words in which the stressed vowel sounds are identical, as are any sounds that follow. Perfect rhyme is predictable, which helps young readers with language development and reading skills.

> **Examples:** *pink/think, hill/bill, sand/hand, house/mouse, cast/fast, book/cook*

In two-syllable words with perfect rhyme, the stressed vowel sounds must still be identical.

> **Examples:** *highlight/skylight, singing/ringing, hokey/pokey, kittens/mittens, itsy/bitsy, tighter/lighter*

Words can also be considered to have perfect rhyme if they are spelled differently, but have the same vowel sound and ending consonant sound.

> **Examples:** crate/eight, near/deer, *moon/June, bear/where, lighter/writer, minor/liner*

Note: For the youngest readers, especially when spelling is important in the learning-to-read process, perfect rhyme with identical spelling is easier for children to read and pronounce.

What is *near rhyme*?
There are different categories of *near rhyme*. Keep in
mind that there is no written rule that says you cannot
use near rhyme, and you will find authors who do
use it (mainly because it affords them more freedom),
however the predictability of perfect rhyme makes it
easier for children to read and pronounce.

Many times, authors feel that near rhyme is close
enough. My feeling is that if something is worth doing,
it's worth doing right. Perfect rhyme is an important
literacy tool, so I believe in going that extra mile for
young readers.

Types of near rhyme to AVOID:
• The final consonants rhyme, but not the vowels
  or initial consonants: walk/click, fun/green,
  sound/pond

• The final consonant sounds are different, but the
  vowel sounds are the same: cat/fact, boot/boost,
  tote/roast, mind/line

• Rhyming a stressed syllable with an unstressed
  syllable: ring/loving, repair/staring, unclear/fearing

• Rhyming a singular word with a plural word:
  tick/clicks, boat/coats, able/tables

• Rhyming a present tense word with a past
  tense word if the past tense word ends with *ed*:
  stalk/walked, time/rhymed, prance/danced

Avoid using words as filler.
If you need a rhyming word to go with a previous line, be sure the word you are using adds value to the story and makes sense. Don't throw in a word that rhymes but has nothing to do with the story.

> **Example:**
> My big brother loves reptiles, especially snakes,
> He also is happy when grandma bakes cakes.

The second line is totally out of context. Try using a different word that rhymes with snakes and also fits the story:

> My big brother loves reptiles, especially snakes,
> I am proud as I watch all the care that he takes.

Avoid convoluted sentences.
If you can't make a word rhyme, don't reorganize the sentence in an unnatural way to find a rhyming word.

> **Example:**
> I love the way we run and play.
> And at your house I will always stay.

Children would not normally say, "at your house I will always stay." You may need to change the first line and try rhyming a different word:

> I love the way we play and run.
> Today we are having so much fun.

Avoid trite rhyming words. Be creative.
There are many over-used rhyming words that are boring and predictable. These are words like day/may/ stay, stop/hop/top, me/see/be.

Experiment with new words, perhaps 2-syllable words. This is where a rhyming dictionary comes in handy. For example, if your character is looking for ways to earn money, simply looking up the word *earning* in the rhyming dictionary offers you words like *learning* and *yearning*. Does that trigger a few new thoughts?

One of my favorite rhyming sites is: www.rhymezone.com

"Think left and think right and think low and think high. Oh, the thinks you can think up if only you try!"
— *Dr. Seuss*

PART 6

Tend to
More Details

29
Choose the
Perfect Title

Every author strives to find the perfect title for their book. Many tend to over-think the process and worry about the title long before they even begin to write; however, deciding on a unique title and then trying to write a book to go with it is not the best way to proceed. If you have a great title in mind, think of it as a *working title,* meaning that the book is a work in progress and so is the title.

That said, a meaningful title *is* of utmost importance to your book. People often *do* judge a book by its cover. The title and cover work hand in hand to form the prospective reader's first impression of the book. When the manuscript is complete, it's important to work with a graphic designer to make sure your title is easy to read.

The job of the title is twofold. It should:
(1) pique the reader's interest.
(2) offer a strong hint as to what the story is about.

In both of these areas, it becomes *your* job to make sure your story lives up to what your title promises.

If you're having trouble deciding on a title, consider the following:

Let your story tell you its title.
I have found that if you wait until the manuscript is written, and you listen carefully, your story will reveal its title. This has nothing to do with magical powers; it has everything to do with the story revealing parts of the main theme that aren't always crystal clear to the writer when the process begins. Often a catchy phrase somewhere in the story will jump out at you and become the perfect title.

Think of your title in terms of keywords.
Keywords are words that shoppers use when searching for specific topics online. This means that you should strive to have keywords in your title that will match common search words. (What words will people Google that will lead them to your book?) Adding a subtitle will enable you to offer even more information about the book, thereby giving you the opportunity to use more keywords. There are a number of online sites where you can find keyword data for every word you search. The more keywords you fit into your title and subtitle, the more discoverable your book will be.

> **Example:** If your book is about a talking truck, the title *Tommy the Talking Truck* will likely show up in the search for children's books about trucks.

If your title is *What Tommy Likes*, you have removed an important keyword and lowered your chances of being discovered in a search.

Things to remember when choosing a title:

• Short and catchy is generally the way to go:
Kittens For Sale, Billy's Bad Day

• Don't give the ending away:
Fluffy Searches For Home, is more intriguing than
Fluffy Finds His Way Home

• Use at least one effective keyword:
*Tommy's Trains and Trucks, The Best Baseball
Game*

• Children love alliteration:
Sammy's Silly Snowy Day, Five Flittering Fairies

• You can pose a puzzling question:
Where Can I Find a Crocodile? Who Ate My Soup?

• A quirky story deserves a quirky title:
Boo Hoo at the Zoo, A Lizard Ate My Basketball

• A lullaby needs a *soft* title:
Sweet Dreams, I Will Kiss You Goodnight

Note: A copyright does not cover the title of a book.
For this reason, you will sometimes see multiple
books with the same title. Even if you have fallen in
love with your title, if you see it on another book, it's
better to come up with a new title of your own, thereby
increasing the chance for your book to stand out and
be discoverable.

W*e don't have to think up a title till we get
the doggone book written."*

—Carl Sandburg

30
How to Paginate
Your Story

Pagination is the process of dividing your completed manuscript into pages. This is the next step, *after* your work has been edited and *before* you begin working with an illustrator. The reason for paginating *after* the edit is that sometimes during a developmental edit, the sequence of events may be altered.

Remember:
Write. Edit. Paginate. Illustrate.

Your goal for each page should be to follow the characters' actions and leave the reader wondering what will happen on the next page.

Know your page count.
You will need to decide how many pages your book will contain before you begin the process of pagination. This number will vary according to the type of book you are writing. A picture book, for example, traditionally consists of 32 pages; this number is derived from the traditional printers' practice of dividing large sheets of paper into 8 pages. However, many self-published authors are choosing to go with page counts of 24, 40, or 48.

If your book is being printed by an offset press, extra pages will usually need to be added in multiples of 4 or 8. (For more information about page count, see *Chapter 3, Types of Children's Books.*)

Keep in mind that in most children's books the story does not begin on page 1. Normally, page 1 is the title page, page 2 the copyright page, and page 3 the dedication page. The story will then begin on page 4, which is the next left-hand page. In a 32-page picture book, you have 24 to 28 pages left for your story, depending on whether or not you wish to add questions, resources, or a glossary at the end of your book.

Follow the process.
I have found the following process useful when dividing a story into pages:

1. Read through your story and create tentative page breaks by putting a small red line after each *action scene*. The goal is to have something happening on each page that is essential to the story, and end each page with a mini cliff-hanger, making the reader anxious to turn to the next page.

2. Then go through the manuscript and adjust the page breaks if necessary, by moving lines of text up to the preceding page or down to the following page, according to the action described. Having one important action on each page will also make it easier to have the illustrations created.

3. Sometimes an author has an idea for an exciting 2-page illustration, or *spread*, that they would like to highlight without any text. For example, a book about the ocean could contain a 2-page spread featuring many ocean creatures in a dramatic underwater panorama—without any words at all. During the pagination process, you can plan for this illustration.

Make a mock-up book.
Another way to paginate is to create a mock-up book, either digitally or with actual paper, scissors and tape. This will allow you to cut and paste, read through the mock-up, and rearrange the order of the text until it feels right. This will help you recognize how the placement of the words can affect the meaning of the story. It will also help you to be sure that each page begins and ends in a logical place.

It's worth reiterating: Follow the action.
Your goal is to have each *page turn* coincide with the words and actions of the characters in order to create true *page-turner experiences*. When you have some type of action taking place on each page, which is imperative in children's books, you will be able to divide the story naturally.

Let the words guide you.
It's okay for some pages to have more words than others. You may also find that there are pages where you can add a bit of page-turning drama by adding a word with an ellipsis at the end of a page. Examples are words such as *Then...* or *She wondered...*

Paginating nonfiction books.
Nonfiction books are often easier to paginate, especially books that feature a type of item (a different seashell, animal, truck, or letter of the alphabet) on each page. In these cases, your decision may simply be how many of the items to feature on each page.

"Turning the page is the only way to get to the next chapter."
—*Billy Cox*

31
Write a Compelling Book Summary

When prospective buyers consider selecting a book, the first thing they look at is the cover—then the title. If their interest is piqued, their next step is usually to turn the book over to read the summary (blurb) on the back. It has long been a belief in the publishing community that most people will read only the first three sentences of the summary before making a decision whether or not they wish to purchase the book. For that reason, the summary should be short, and should contain a *hook* to grab the readers' attention and make them want more.

The longer your summary, the less likely it is that people will read it. Your goals should be to capture the essence of the story in as few sentences as possible, highlight the key ideas, and keep the descriptive words to a minimum. Make it a bit mysterious if you can, and never tell the entire story! If you tell your prospective readers what happens in the beginning, middle and end, you have revealed too much, possibly leaving them with no reason to buy the book.

Write your summary in a tone that reflects the feel of your story. For example, if your book is silly, add a bit of silliness to your summary. If your book is a bedtime lullaby, use soothing words that reflect the quiet mood of the story.

Important note: It is imperative that your summary be free of grammatical and/or spelling errors. This important paragraph offers insight into your ability to write, so have your editor look at it to be sure it is clear, effective, and free of mistakes.

Following are a few sample *before* and *after* book summaries to guide you:

Before:
The storyline of this book is about a boy named Ethan who is a bright but shy third grader, and is really a bit nerdy. He is known as a nerdy kid because all he likes to do is read. He always talks about one day becoming a dog trainer. Besides possessing a wild imagination, Ethan loves to create unusual inventions. When the principal, Mr. Burke, announces a school science contest where the winner will get free ice cream at lunch for a month, Ethan finally finds an opportunity to show his classmates and teacher how smart he really is. He works frantically every night, coming up with an amazing invention that takes his classmates and teacher by storm. He creates the very first insulated spacesuit for dogs that will make it possible for them to walk on the moon. **(140 words)**

After:
Ethan is a shy student with dreams of becoming a dog trainer. His love of reading, along with his hobby of constructing unusual inventions, creates the perfect combination of imagination and determination. His amazing idea drives the story forward as he vows to create the most original entry in his class science contest. **(53 words)**

Before:
Katie has always wanted to learn to ride a horse. After all, her friend Alice rides all the time and she says it's very easy. But horses are so big and Katie is very nervous. She is encouraged by her instructor who keeps telling her she really can do it. Then one day a group of Katie's friends shows up at her riding lesson. They all cheer her on and tell her she can do it. Finally Katie relaxes and is able to ride around the ring without any help from her instructor. She learns that bravery comes from love, kindness, and encouragement from those you trust. **(107 words)**

After:
Katie tries to overcome her fears while still enjoying the adventure of learning to ride a horse. The courage she gains from her instructor and friends provides the boost she needs. Katie learns that bravery comes from love, kindness, and encouragement from those you trust. **(47 words)**

Before:
Johnny goes to his grandma's house for a sleepover visit. His three cousins also come along for the fun. No one knows that Johnny walks in his sleep, so when it happens, his cousins really aren't sure what to do. First they try to wake him up, but that doesn't work. Then they try very hard to keep him in bed by blocking the door. Finally, they try walking him back to his bed and piling lots of blankets on top of him. Have they finally solved their problem? Will they finally get him to stay in his bed or will he wander around all night? **(106 words)**

After:
When Johnny comes for an overnight visit, his hilarious sleepwalking antics keep everyone scrambling to keep him in bed. This zany story is perfect for young children who love to have fun. Readers will giggle as Johnny's night wanderings lead to some strange situations. **(44 words)**

Before:
Once there were three very unlikely friends—a cat, a fox and a very strange mouse named Lola. They liked to travel around at night because it is really quiet after dark, and anyway they can all see very well in the dark. They build friendship and teamwork as these strange night visitors solve some very unpredictable mysteries that occur during the night. They find a very strange object that they think might have fallen from the sky. Finally they discover the truth and make it back home safely before the sun comes up. **(94 words)**

After:
Three unlikely friends—a cat, a fox, and a peculiar mouse—are out to solve a mystery. Join the *night travelers* team as they unravel the secret of a strange object that has landed on Earth. **(36 words)**

Remember: Make it short. Offer a hint. Make the prospective reader want to know more!

'The most valuable of all talents is that of never using two words when one will do."
—Thomas Jefferson

32
Write a Credible Bio

Your personal bio is an important part of your book. After prospective buyers look at the cover, title and summary, the next thing they will read is your bio. Since they now know what the story is about, they are interested in learning who wrote the book. Your bio can completely alter the way someone views the book—for better or worse.

Remember, the prospective reader may be a rushed buyer or an impatient child. Capture their attention quickly, just as you did with the summary. The shorter the bio, the more likely people are to read it.

Always write the bio in third person.
Always, always, always introduce yourself in third person.

> **Incorrect:** I am the author of the series, *All About Cats.*
> **Correct:** Jane Doe is the author of the series, *All About Cats.*

Begin with credibility. Ask yourself what aspect of your background will connect with your readers. They want to know what gives you the credibility to write this book and why they should believe your words.

If you have a college degree, it's important to highlight the fact that you are well educated; however, after mentioning your degree, or degrees, do not ramble on by listing all of your life's achievements. This is not the place for a full resume.

People generally are not interested in your education if it has nothing to do with your topic or genre. For example, if you are an optometrist, you may be the perfect person to write a story about a child who is embarrassed about wearing glasses, but your degree would add no credibility to a story about baking cupcakes.

If you have written a bedtime rhyming story, your multiple degrees in science and technology won't really matter to a potential reader. On the other hand, if you also have years of daycare experience, highlighting that aspect of your life is important. Your credibility might simply be that you have lessons to share that you have learned from your own children, or you may want to highlight the interest you have always had in the subject you are writing about.

Tell the prospective buyer what inspired you to write your book and how your life relates and contributes to the story you have written. What experiences have you had that you feel have contributed to your knowledge and understanding of the topic?

Examples:

- Jimmy Jones has worked as a circus clown for 20 years.
- John Smith was bullied throughout most of his childhood.
- As a kindergarten teacher, Jane Doe understands the importance of teaching young children about food allergies.

Mention other successful books you have written.

It is a helpful marketing strategy to mention other books you have written in the same genre. You can also mention awards, award nominations, and media attention; but be sure they are credible awards and media sources. If this is your first book, after mentioning your credentials, it is fine to say: *This is his first published story,* or *In her debut children's book...*

Examples:

- Jimmy Jones is best known for his award-winning children's book, *Everyone Loves a Clown.*
- John Smith is the author of the award-nominated book, *I Believe in Me.*
- Jane Doe's previous book, *No Peanuts For Me,* has been featured in numerous blogs and online news articles relating to food allergies in children.

State your ultimate goal.
Reach out to your readers by telling them your goal in writing the story. If prospective buyers connect with your goal and find it intriguing, they will be more likely to accompany you on your adventure.

Examples:

- Jimmy's goal in writing this book is to highlight the outlandish fun and excitement of training to be a clown.
- John shows how believing in himself helped him end bullying in his school.
- Jane knows her story will resonate with children who are living with food allergies.

Be positive.
Don't ever say, "Jimmy *hopes* readers will like this book." Instead, say, "Jimmy *knows* circus lovers will find this book hilarious."

End with something personal—even comical.
Examples:

- Jimmy lives in Colorado, where he enjoys *clowning around* on the ski slopes with his wife and three children.
- John is the proud father of three boys, who are also committed to ending bullying.
- Jane loves to create allergy-free treats for her three children.

Let's Put the Bios Together

Using the information in the examples above, let's create a few bios:
• Jimmy Jones has worked as a circus clown for 20 years. He is best known for his award-winning children's book, *Everyone Loves a Clown*. His goal in writing this book is to highlight the outlandish fun and excitement of training to be a clown. Jimmy lives in Colorado, where he enjoys *clowning around* on the ski slopes with his wife and children.

• John Smith was bullied throughout most of his childhood. He is the author of the award-nominated book, *I Believe in Me*. John openly shares the ways that believing in himself helped him end bullying in his school. John is the proud father of three boys, who are also committed to ending bullying.

• As a kindergarten teacher, Jane Doe understands the importance of teaching young children about food allergies. Her previous book, *No Peanuts For Me,* has been featured in numerous blogs and online news articles about food allergies in children. She knows her story will resonate with children who are living with allergies. Jane loves to create allergy-free treats for her three children.

Note: Avoid beginning every sentence with the author's name. After you have constructed the bio, alternate the name with a pronoun in some of the sentences. Don't begin every sentence with *Jane did...* Instead, change a few to *She did...*

More Sample Author Bios

Jane Doe is a licensed family therapist in private practice in Florida and presently teaches courses in family resilience. Her goal is to share the knowledge she has gained from her experiences with children, parents and educators, and to enable children to better understand and control their feelings. Jane enjoys spending time with her pets, including her turtle, Tommy.

Jason Jones is a full-time single dad on a mission to write books that help make parenting easier. His love for reading began when he was a child; he later became motivated to write his own stories to read to his sons. When not working on his electronic devices, Jason can be found cooking for his kids. You can follow his parenting journey on his website.

Bobbie Hinman has a B.S. degree in Elementary Education/Children's Literature. The combination of her teaching experience and time spent with her thirteen grandchildren has given her insight into the way children think. Bobbie has been a speaker at numerous schools, libraries and book festivals. She is currently in demand as an editor of children's books.

Sample Contributor Bios

If you have room on your book jacket or marketing material for a bio of your illustrator or graphic designer, be sure to help them adhere to the same goals and format—short and to the point. It's also a good idea to have your editor check the contributors' bios to make sure they are free of errors.

Illustrator:
Jane Doe attended Maryland Institute College of Art where she gained the knowledge and experience necessary to work in her chosen field as a children's book illustrator. Her original watercolor illustrations are captivating, making this magical story come alive. Jane is actively involved with her two loves—children and the arts.

Graphic designer:
John Smith has a Bachelor of Fine Arts degree in Communication Arts and is an accomplished art director and graphic designer. Throughout his career, he has designed books covering a wide variety of subjects; however, he has discovered that he gains the most enjoyment from designing children's books.

"Great geniuses have the shortest biographies."
—Ralph Waldo Emerson

PART 7

Revise and Perfect Your Manuscript

33

Revise, Rewrite and Troubleshoot

So you have written your story and that's that, right?
I'm afraid not. Few among us have the insight and
ability to write a story in one sitting, or one week, or
one month... so don't be too hard on yourself if you've
been working on your story for a while and just can't
seem to get it right. Writing a book is a *process* that
is not accomplished leisurely in one afternoon. Most
of the authors I queried said they had revised—or
completely rewritten—their children's book between
five and ten times, the length of time varying from one
month to three years, or even longer.

Keep in mind that the first audience you have should
be *you*. Read your work out loud and see if it makes
sense to you. Words sound different when you read
them out loud. You will hear the sound of your writer's
voice—an important step in the process. Reading out
loud will also help you eliminate clunky sentences and
unneeded punctation, and it will give you a feel for
how your audience will receive your language.

The next step is to have someone else read it *to* you.
This is a good way for you to listen for awkward spots
or any confusing wording in the story.

If you detect something that doesn't sound right, do not ignore it, even though it's sometimes simpler to tell yourself that it's not that big of a deal. Identify the problem. It's better to fix it now than to publish an imperfect story.

Here are some guidelines to consider when analyzing your manuscript:

Is my idea relevant?

Is my story relatable?

Is the opening sentence enticing?

Is each sentence clear and coherent?

Are my characters interesting?

Is there enough dialogue?

Is there too much dialogue?

Is the vocabulary appropriate?

Is the story too wordy?

Are the spelling and grammar correct?

Is the tense the same throughout the story?

Does the plot have a conflict with resolution?

Is the plot direct or does it wander?

Is there an identifiable beginning, middle and end?

Is there action on every page?

Is there enough action?

Is the situation resolved?

Is the end satisfying?

Does the rhyme work?

Have I forced any words to rhyme?

Is the rhyming meter consistent?

If there's an issue, each of these areas can be remedied. Go back and reread the chapter in this book that deals with each problem. When you feel confident about your manuscript, it's time for a few beta readers—and then a professional edit.

"When your story is ready for rewrite, cut it to the bone. Get rid of every bit of excess fat. This is going to hurt; revising a story down to the bare essentials is always a little like murdering children, but it must be done."
—Stephen King

34

The Role of a
Beta Reader

Hiring an editor comes with a price; beta readers are usually free. But don't be confused—beta readers are NOT replacements for professional editors. Even knowing this, it's sometimes too easy for new writers to rely on beta readers for their main source of feedback throughout the entire writing process. This is not a good idea! A beta reader is not intended to play the role of an editor, and if you go this route, you run the risk of overlooking potential flaws in your manuscript.

Keep in mind that the main scope of the critique from a beta reader is often coming from an amateur's point of view. This means that if you rely too heavily on beta readers for your editing needs, you are, in most cases, relying on nonprofessionals to help you create a professionally-written manuscript.

That being said, beta readers *can* play an important role in the writing process by giving you general feedback about your manuscript. Their role should be to read your story and make sure that what you intended to have there *is* there—an interesting plot, relatable characters, and a clear message or theme.

Beta readers can offer feedback from a consumer's point of view and give you an idea of how prospective readers will likely respond to your book. If the beta readers notice errors, they should point them out, but they should not make changes to your story. If you are not sure if your plot is working or if your main character's point of view is coming across, you may want to ask your beta readers what they think about a specific issue. Just be careful not to let them become a crutch.

You may be lucky enough to find beta readers who are familiar with the writing process and are able to provide deeper thoughts on storyline, character, dialogue, etc. But for the most part, you need them to focus on how appealing they find the story and whether or not it makes sense.

The ideal time for a beta reader to enter into the process is just before your story is professionally edited. This gives you time to make any necessary changes before you send it to an editor; but only make these changes if you agree with them and feel that this will strengthen your story. If you send your manuscript to beta readers too early, and depend on them to help *create* your story, you will likely end up totally confused. You may be left with a story that reflects too many voices and isn't at all what you had intended.

How many beta readers should you use?
There is no magic number. Choosing the best adult beta readers takes a lot of thought. You may be able to connect with a few librarians, elementary teachers, or daycare providers. Three to five adults and two

groups of youngsters will usually give you sufficient feedback. For young beta readers, try neighborhood kids, elementary schools, libraries, daycare centers, cub scout and brownie troops, etc.

How to Select Your Beta Readers

Your target audience
The ideal beta readers are in your target audience. What better indication is there of how your intended readers will respond to your book than reading it to a group of your intended readers? This does not mean that you should use *only* children as beta readers. But in my experience, their feedback has consistently been more useful—and insightful—than that of many of my adult beta readers. A combination of the two is ideal.

Parents of your target age group
This is often a good group to ask. They are likely more knowledgeable about children's books than many other adults, and they know what their children like to read.

Other writers
Maybe. If they have had enough experience with the writing process, other writers will understand the challenges of creating a book and may offer some constructive advice. However, if their level of experience is the same as yours, they may not be able to help you, except to say whether or not they like the story.

Friends

While many writers are proud to share their work with friends, this may not always be the best choice for choosing beta readers. Friends and family members often feel tentative about offering advice, thereby not giving honest feedback. Although they mean well, they are often afraid of hurting your feelings. In addition, friends and relatives are usually not qualified to offer a valid manuscript critique. While they may have a feeling that a story isn't working, few are able to pinpoint specifics that can truly help you improve your story. They may not have the understanding needed to identify issues with the plot, dialogue, character development, or forward movement.

How to Glean the Most Information From Your Youngest Beta Readers

I can't stress enough the importance of seeking the children's perspective. In most cases, you will need to read the story to them. A good way to begin is to ask the children to close their eyes and imagine the scene and main character that you are about to describe. Set the stage for the youngsters, using descriptive words to help them visualize the characters and action. Then have them open their eyes and listen to the story. You can even bring along sketches or clipart to give them an idea of what your characters look like.

After reading the story, ask the following types of questions:

- What did you learn from this story?
- What did you like best about the story?
- Is there any character that you would like to be?
- Is there any character that didn't seem important?
- What would you add to the story?
- What would you leave out of the story?
- What would you change to make the story better?
- Would you change the ending? How?

The answer to these questions will tell you whether or not the story delivered your intended message. Notice that I didn't suggest simply asking if they liked or disliked the story. You are not looking for approval; you are asking for constructive ideas to make your story better. Be sure to glance at the children while you read; it's easy to tell by their expressions exactly how they feel. Hint: Eyes rolling back in their heads indicates boredom.

Be sure to listen carefully to what your beta readers have to say. Weigh their suggestions carefully. If you feel their ideas are valid and will enhance your plot or dialogue, take the time to make the changes in your manuscript before sending it off to the editor. If you're not sure, consult with your editor about the suggested changes *before* beginning the process. It's unfair to an editor to send your manuscript to beta readers *after* the edit is complete and ask the editor to make all the changes that the beta readers suggested.

"Too many cooks spoil the broth."
—Early proverb

35
Understanding the Editing Process

To begin with, *you* are your first editor.

After *you* have reviewed and approved your manuscript, it is time to:

* review the feedback of a few beta readers.
* consult with a focus group of children in your target audience.
* make any changes that you feel are essential to your story.

Once you have completed these steps, it's time to hire an editor.

Every story needs a pair of professional eyes to look at the manuscript in its entirety from a fresh perspective. You may be familiar with Abraham Lincoln's famous expression referring to lawyers: *He who represents himself has a fool for a client.* This can also be applied to writers who edit their own books. Even if you have a background in literature, or you have been an English teacher for many years, you need an editor. It's too easy to miss mistakes when proofreading your own work; your eyes tend to skip errors, often seeing what you *think* is there.

Please DO NOT make the mistake of having your book illustrated until *after* your manuscript has been edited. During a comprehensive edit, the order of the story may change, the characters' roles may be altered, or sections of text may even be omitted. This process can become overly complicated if the editor is forced to work around existing illustrations.

There is nothing more valuable than professional feedback.
Editors are well worth the cost and can save you money in the long run. All writers, not only first-timers, should value professional feedback that will help make their work the best it can be.

Don't fret about having your feelings hurt.
Don't resist hiring an editor because you are afraid of being criticized. Constructive criticism of your work is *not* a criticism of *you*. Editors understand that you have put a lot of hard work into your manuscript, and their goal is not to attack it. If you listen to what they have to say, and remain objective, you will realize that their goal is to make your story better.

If you disagree with a change that your editor has made, it's appropriate to ask for an explanation. This will usually be followed by a discussion of how to come up with an acceptable solution. Your willingness to have your story revised is an important area to discuss with your editor at the start of the process.

Do your homework when selecting an editor.
If you are writing a children's book, it's imperative to
choose an editor who specializes in editing children's
books. These experienced editors have read hundreds
and hundreds of children's books and manuscripts,
and have possibly written a few themselves.

Don't be shy about asking prospective editors for
several references, along with information about:

- their educational background as it pertains
  to editing.
- their years of experience.
- the type of editing they offer.
- whether or not they work with rhyme and
  verse (if you are writing a rhyming story).

Types of Editing

Editing is not a *one size fits all* type of process. There
are different types of edits, each dealing with a specific
area of the writing process.

Developmental edit
A developmental edit, also called a structural or substantive edit, will look at the story in its entirety and focus on the overall structure, as well as many other important components. The focus is on the organization, style and consistency of all aspects of the story development. This part of the editing process must come first—before trying to correct the grammar and punctuation. A developmental edit deals with the following aspects:

- Is the plot well developed?
- Have the characters been properly developed?
- Does the story arc need strengthening?
- Does each page have a *hook* that encourages forward movement?
- Is there enough dialogue, and is it used properly?
- Is the tense the same throughout the story?
- Is the sentence structure correct?
- Does your message come through?
- Is the language appropriate for your target audience?

Line edit
A line edit focuses on the language, writing style, and sentence structure of your story. A line edit considers the following aspects:
- Are you overusing certain words?
- Are you using run-on sentences rather than concise sentences?
- Is the meaning of *each* sentence clear?

Copy edit

A copy edit focuses on the spelling, punctuation and capitalization of your story. This is obviously a task that should take place at the very end of the editing process.

If you are only receiving a line edit or copy edit, your story may be missing out on some important structural work.

Looking at the Big Picture: Comprehensive Edit

A comprehensive edit looks at the manuscript in its totality. Editors who offer a comprehensive edit usually include developmental, line, *and* copy editing in one edit. Working with one editor saves you the cost of hiring three different editors; plus, the entire process usually runs more smoothly than working with several people who may have different approaches and perspectives.

Ask questions and be sure you know what type of edit you are paying for. Keep in mind that an editor is a trained professional. We expect to pay professionals for their expertise and their time; editing is no different.

"You can't train for something all your life and then have it fall short because you are hurrying to get it finished."
—John Steinbeck

36

Preparing for the Illustration Process

There's no doubt about it—the success of a children's book, especially a picture book, often relies largely on the illustrations. For the young audience, pictures offer a visual narrative that is necessary if the reader is to fully understand the story. I describe the entire illustration process in my book, *How to Create a Successful Children's Picture Book;* however, there are a few things you need to think about *during* the writing process that will help make the illustration phase go smoothly.

How The Illustrations Support Your Words

Illustrations clarify the meaning of the text.
For the youngest readers, those who are just beginning to enjoy board books, the illustrations help the children's developing brains learn to decode the words. The visual experience helps children make meaning out of the written symbols. For example, children start by seeing the word *ball,* along with an illustration of a ball. After seeing this a few times, when they see the word *ball* by itself, they will visualize a ball. This is how reading begins.

For slightly older readers, whose comprehension skills are continually developing, illustrations give additional meaning to the words. For example, if a story mentions a weeping willow tree, the illustration will most likely be essential to the readers' total understanding.

Illustrations elaborate and add meaning to the story.
Illustrations can save you a lot of words. Any location that is unfamiliar to children can be better understood with an illustration. In stories that take place in another country, or under the sea, or on another planet, most children will not have a point of reference without illustrations. Even for middle grade readers, a complicated item or concept can often be made more understandable with an illustration.

If you are writing a nonfiction book about a topic such as sea creatures, no amount of explanation can describe something as complex as a lobster without the help of a picture.

Illustrations can even augment a story by showcasing a character who is never even mentioned in the story. An example from one of my own books is a mouse who is not mentioned in the story of The Knot Fairy, but is seen throughout the book with knots in its tail, adding another element of fun to the story.

Illustrations can offer clues.
For an added element of mystery, the illustrations can offer silent clues. A character with a lost hat can be seen looking high and low on every page. The hat can appear, unmentioned, in every illustration, even though the character doesn't see it. This can provide

an exciting experience as the reader sees the missing hat and cheers for the character.

Illustrations help create a feeling or mood.
Illustrations can help offer an immediate indication of the mood of the story. An illustration of a dreary, rainy day offers a different feeling than one of bright sunlight. An illustration of Grandma's comfy living room will give the reader a feeling quite different from a scene in a haunted house. Using illustrations effectively is an important element that many authors neglect. When planning the illustrations, be sure to pay strict attention, not only to the characters, but also to their surroundings and the overall feel of the story. Once you have these aspects in mind, you will need to share your thoughts with your illustrator. These are some of the details that you will work out together.

Illustrations add color—and are fun to look at.
They enhance the reading experience, make it more enjoyable, and encourage children's overall enjoyment of art.

Planning the Illustrations

Begin with your initial idea.
You are probably picturing the scenes in your mind the minute the story idea first pops into your head. As you develop the characters and storyline, you can take notes about what the characters are doing and where the scenes take place. You might even know what your characters are wearing.

Recognize that your ideas are fluid.
As you add to your ideas and notes, recognize that these notes are *fluid,* meaning that they will change as the story evolves. Let the story guide the illustrations.

Look for an illustrator who shares your vision.
As your story progresses and the editing process is in sight, you can begin your search for an illustrator. Take your time, look at books online and in bookstores, and find an illustration style that appeals to you. It's a good idea to have a few illustrators show you examples of how they would depict your main character.

Turn your words into pictures.
Once your story has been professionally edited, it's time to actually begin the illustration process. Let the story guide you. The words on each page should be depicted by an illustration that reflects what the words are saying. For example, if the words say that Billy is fishing with his dad, the illustration should show them fishing. If your story takes place at night, don't show a sunlit sky.

Pay attention to the background. A generic background looks like a generic background. When planning the illustrations, plan the setting for each page. This doesn't mean the background has to change on each page; you can have more than one action take place in the same room. You can also add elements, change the angle, or make some of the illustrations closeups.

Plan the action.
Plan the action for each page. Avoid static pictures, such as scenery without characters. Each illustration, like each page of text, should show action. Also avoid having stiff-looking characters who are simply standing in the same position on every page. If you find that there is nothing to show on a page because nothing new is happening, this is an important message to you that the story probably needs more action.

Always plan to have the action in the illustrations move from left to right. This will help the flow of the story. On the left-hand page, the action will drive readers to the right-hand page. On the right-hand page, the action will drive readers to turn to the next page.

Show expressions.
Showing expressions on your characters' faces is of utmost importance in children's books. You can also eliminate unnecessary words in the text by having the characters' facial expressions show the reader how the characters are feeling. Keep this in mind when you search for an illustrator. When requesting sample drawings, ask to see samples of characters with a variety of expressions.

Some editors will help you break your story down into pages. Having these page breaks *before* the illustrator begins working on your book will make the process run smoother for everyone. *(See Chapter 23, How to Paginate Your Story.)*

Ask traditional publishers what they prefer.
If you are planning to submit your manuscript to a traditional publisher, it may be best to not have it illustrated. In many cases, the publisher will want to choose the illustrator. Do your research and find out what the publisher prefers. If you are working with a literary agent, they will often be able to provide some information for you about the preferences of specific publishers.

"Illustrations have as much to say as the text. The trick is to say the same thing, but in a different way."
—*Maurice Sendak*

Let the story guide the illustrations.

PART 8

A Few
Last Words

37

Epilogue:
I Will Leave You With
These Thoughts

Enjoy the sound of language and the feelings these
sounds create.

Choose your words wisely.

Find joy in being creative.

Use language to unlock the imagination.

Be sincere in your desire to communicate.

Always write from your heart.

Most importantly, have fun!

*"Be yourself; everyone else is already
taken."*
                                        —Oscar Wilde

Acknowledgements

Writing a book is not an easy process. Writers often face daunting challenges as they yearn to share their ideas and messages with the world.

This book is about helping—the people I have helped and those who have helped me. Writing may at times be a lonely art; if we help each other, the journey can be joyful—and even exhilarating.

I want to send a heartfelt, special thank you to those who have helped me in my mission to help you:

Dr. Seuss, in his special library in Heaven, whose books taught me at a young age to think in rhyme.

Joann Sky,[1] my outstanding editor, for her wonderful ideas and suggestions, and for helping me get my message across in just the right amount of words. Her knowledge and experience have been invaluable.

Jeff Urbancic,[2] my graphic designer extraordinaire, who has been with me on every single project. He performed magic on my children's books and still smiles when I ask him to make "just one more teensy change."

Kristi Bridgeman,[3] for being with me from the start and teaching me to find the perfect balance between words and pictures. Her incredible fairy illustrations brought my ideas to life.

Louie Romares, for his patience and creativity in designing the perfect cover.

Ruth Maille and **Rachel Hilz**, my astute beta readers, for their thorough job and thoughtful suggestions.

Gloria Purwin, my dear friend indeed, who is always willing to lend an educated pair of eyes.

My husband **Harry**, for being my business partner and best friend and for always being there, even when the odds seemed overwhelming. I'm so happy I created you!

My precious grandchildren, the creators and designers of my journey. My fairy books would never have existed without your inspiration. I love you to the moon and back—and more!

[1]JoAnn Sky is a multi-genre published author—and a certified copy editor—who has been writing and editing professionally for years. She authors adult contemporary romance, young adult romance with a magical twist, and children's books. She is an experienced editor of both fiction (adult and children's/ middle grade) and non-fiction (self-help, business and academic) books. Originally from the Midwest, JoAnn currently lives in northern Nevada with her own happily-ever-after: her husband, three children, and three crazy rescue dogs. To learn more about her books and editing services, visit www.joannsky.com.

[2]Jeff Urbancic has a Bachelor of Fine Arts degree in Communications Arts. He is an accomplished art director and graphic designer. He has designed books covering a variety of subjects; however, he gains the most enjoyment out of designing children's books. Jeff lives in Virginia with his wife and two children. He can be contacted through The Urbancic Creative Group, LLC at: jurbancic5@comcast.net.

[3]Kristi Bridgeman resides on Vancouver Island, B.C., Canada. Known for her sepia tones and glowing lines, some of her work has been said to resemble that of Victorian children's illustrators. She has illustrated numerous children's books and has been honored as one of the 150 Top Women Artists through the Federation of Canadian Artists. Her work can be seen at: www.kristibridgeman.com.

About the Author

Bobbie Hinman is the author of the successful bestseller, *How to Create a Successful Children's Book,* in which she delves into the topics of self-publishing and marketing. Bobbie's five children's picture books, *The Knot Fairy, The Sock Fairy, The Belly Button Fairy, The Fart Fairy* and *The Freckle Fairy* have received a combined total of twenty-eight children's book awards. Bobbie is currently in demand as an editor of children's books.

Growing up in Baltimore, Maryland, Bobbie graduated from Towson University with a B.S. degree in Elementary Education and a minor in Children's Literature. As an elementary teacher, she kept abreast of the world of children's books, always encouraging reading as a path to a successful future. She always knew deep down that someday she would write a children's book...or two...or three...

Bobbie and her husband Harry have always believed in following a healthy lifestyle and, for this reason, raised their children on a farm with horses, golden retrievers, cats, chickens, and a goat named Timothy. An advocate of healthy eating, Bobbie is the author and co-author of seven successful cookbooks.

Bobbie recently penned a narrative memoir about her family's life on the farm—and the ghost who was there long before they arrived. In *The Ghost of My Lady's Memoir,* she shares their real-life experiences.

Bobbie has been a speaker and presenter at numerous schools, libraries and bookstores, as well as major book festivals and fairy festivals all across the United States and in Canada. Her articles have appeared in the Independent Book Publishers Association magazine and in many blogs and interviews. Bobbie's bookstore events have been featured in the *Barnes & Noble Inside* newsletter.

Bobbie and her husband Harry live in Florida with their two kitties, Twinkle and Boo. Their children are now grown, and the Hinmans are the proud grandparents of thirteen grandchildren, all of whom played significant roles in the development of the Fairy Book Series. None of this would ever have happened without them!

Also by Bobbie Hinman

The Knot Fairy
The Sock Fairy
The Belly Button Fairy
The Fart Fairy
The Freckle Fairy

Best Fairy Books Picture Book Treasury

(Fairy book versions: hardcover, paperback,
e-books and coloring books)

How to Create a Successful Children's Picture Book

The Ghost of My Lady's Manor

Best Fairy Books

Bestfairybooks.com

Index

narrator, role of, 113

nonfiction books
   creative nonfiction, 141
   definition, 137
   STEM, 138

·O·
opening sentence, make it inviting, 97

outline, how to create, 43

·P·
paginating (page breaks), how to, 211

picture books, characteristics, 25

·R·
reading, what children like, 17

rhyme
   anapestic meter, 179
   understanding meter, 175
   iambic meter, 185
   metric patterns, 175
   pitfalls of, 199
   rhyme punctuation, 193
   rhyme scheme, 169
   to rhyme or not to rhyme, 159

·S·
sentences, how to write, 57

series, how to create, 145

Made in United States
North Haven, CT
18 March 2022